TEACHER'S MANUAL BOOK 2

Basic Skills in English

McDougal, Littell & Company
Evanston, Illinois

This Teacher's Manual was prepared with the assistance of

Susan Duffy Schaffrath

Donna Rae Blackall

Editorial Director: Joy Littell
Editorial Coordinator: Kathleen Laya
Associate Editor: Patricia Opaskar
Director of Design: William Seabright
Associate Designer: Lucy Lesiak

ISBN: 0-88343-769-4

CONTENTS

Special Features of *Basic Skills in English*

Scope and Purpose of the Series

Basic Skills in English is an English series for grades 7-12 designed to help students master essential writing and other language skills. The series is suitable for students of all ability levels, but is particularly appropriate for students reading below grade level. While each successive book in the series takes into account the increasing maturity of the student, the reading level remains within the fifth- to sixth-grade range. This text (Book 2) is recommended for use at grade 8. It has a fifth-grade reading level.

Organization of Each Book

Each book in the series is divided into two main parts:

1. **Composition.** The first half of the book includes sections on vocabulary development, sentence improvement, and the writing of paragraphs, compositions, and letters. It also includes sections on those skills that support the student in writing and editing his or her own work: dictionary use, library use, and the use of important reference works.

2. **Handbook.** The second half of the book includes sections on grammar and usage, capitalization, punctuation, and spelling.

Key Features of the COMPOSITION Part (pages 2-63)

1. **The lessons follow a simple, consistent plan.** Each lesson deals with a single topic or skill and is short enough (usually two pages) to insure completion of the instruction in one class period. The students follow this plan for each lesson:

Here's the Idea This presents to the students the idea or skill to be learned in the lesson.

Check It Out The students react to the idea, and test it to be sure that they understand it.

Try Your Skill The students apply the idea or skill in a short structured exercise.

Keep This in Mind A boxed summary reinforces the students' understanding of the main idea of the lesson.

Now Write The students perform an independent writing assignment for which they are now well prepared.

2. **The lessons emphasize the steps in the process of writing.** Writing is a mystery for many students; they do not understand what is expected of them. In these lessons the students can actually see the development of a piece of writing. The lessons move from selecting a topic, listing specific details, organizing notes, writing a draft, revising and editing, to making a final copy. This step-by-step process unravels the mysteries of writing and helps students to achieve a satisfying measure of success in composition.

3. **The lessons are progressive.** Within each book the instruction moves from work with smaller units of writing to larger units. It moves from choosing the right word (vocabulary development) to writing sentences, to writing paragraphs, to writing a composition or a report. Within each section, it follows closely the steps in the process of writing, recognizing the students' need to know how to begin a piece of writing, how to develop it, and how to complete it. Within each lesson, it moves from an explanation of an idea to its application.

4. **The lessons are practical.** The skills and techniques presented are useful to the student now and in later life. They have been selected specifically for their utility. The examples that illustrate them and the assignments that provide practice on them

have been chosen to demonstrate how they can help the student in both academic and work settings.

5. **The lessons are illustrated with many examples.** These include not only examples of finished work but also examples of work at various stages in the process of writing, so that the students can see at first hand what is expected as an end result. The examples present work that the students can expect to equal, not work so far beyond their abilities that it intimidates more than it inspires.

6. **The lessons are organized to insure success.** The students are never asked to do something that has not been taught. Furthermore, exercises based on a concept or skill do not require that the students have fully mastered the concept or skill. The tone of the instruction throughout is one of encouragement, reflecting confidence in the students' abilities.

Key Features of the HANDBOOK Part (Pages 65-140)

1. **The Handbook part of *Basic Skills in English* presents a clear, comprehensive treatment of grammar, usage, capitalization, punctuation, and spelling.** The text is organized for direct teaching; it is also organized in such a way that students can easily use the Handbook independently for reference.

2. **Each Section is a self-contained unit.** Each section is devoted to a single topic, and all information on that topic is presented together in the Section. Everything about nouns is presented in one Section, everything about pronouns in another Section, and so on.

3. **Each Section has a wealth of exercises.** Every Section is divided into Parts, each Part dealing with a separate skill. Each Part concludes with exercises on the skill developed. Wherever possible, there are several exercises using a variety of approaches to the same skill. Each Section is followed by a cumulative review of all the skills developed in that Section. This quantity and variety of exercises provides the teacher with ample material for practice, reinforcement, and review.

4. **The typographic arrangement is clear and attractive.** Type and open space have been used to set off definitions and examples so as to make them easy to find and easy to read.

This Teacher's Manual

There are three sections in the Teacher's Manual:

1. **This Introduction,** entitled "Special Features of *Basic Skills in English.*"

2. **Teaching Suggestions for Composition (pages 2-54) and Teaching Suggestions for the Handbook (pages 55-146).** The Teaching Suggestions include these elements:

Section Objectives This is a list of the skills that each student is expected to master in the study of the Section.

Preparing the Students This is a lesson designed to orient the students to the subject of the Section.

Presenting the Lesson These are step-by-step suggestions for teaching each Part in the Section, stressing points of emphasis and offering suggestions for use of the exercises.

Optional Practice This is an additional teaching resource for drill or review of materials.

Extending the Lesson This is an enrichment lesson or exercise relating the material discussed in the Part to a new topic, or approaching the material in a new way.

3. **Keys to Exercises.** These begin on page 147.

Related Materials

Besides the exercises provided in the student text and the Teacher's Manual, additional supporting materials are available. These are coordinated with the Sections in *Basic Skills in English, Book 1.*

Skills Practice Book This consumable workbook provides additional practice and reinforcement keyed to the Sections in the text.

Diagnostic and Mastery Tests This consumable booklet includes pretests for Sections for which students may be expected to have prior learning, and mastery tests for all Sections. These tests enable the teacher to assess student needs before presenting a Section, and to determine any needs for reviewing afterwards.

Basic Skills in English

Book 6 — Recommended for grade 12

Book 5 — Recommended for grade 11

Book 4 — Recommended for grade 10

Book 3 — Recommended for grade 9

Book 2 — Recommended for grade 8

Book 1 — Recommended for grade 7

TEACHING SUGGESTIONS FOR

Basic Skills in English

BOOK 2

Words: Developing Your Vocabulary

Pages 1-17

Objectives

1. To become acquainted with the many sources of English words
2. To increase awareness of English as a changing language
3. To understand the use of context clues in learning word meanings
4. To use the direct context clues of definition and restatement to learn word meanings
5. To recognize examples used as context clues
6. To study the use of comparison and contrast as context clues
7. To understand the importance of using precise words to express ideas
8. To learn to recognize base words
9. To understand the meanings and use of common prefixes
10. To understand the meanings and use of common suffixes

Preparing the Students

Contrast the vocabulary needed by early cave dwellers with the highly complex vocabulary needed by people today. Explain that language development has paralleled the development of civilization. Emphasize the value of studying the origins, use, and structure of words as a method of extending vocabulary.

Part 1 **Alive and Well** Using Our Language pp. 2-3

Objectives 1. To become acquainted with the many sources of English words

2. To increase awareness of English as a changing language

Presenting the Lesson 1. Read aloud and discuss *Here's the Idea.* Draw a time line on the chalkboard to show the progression from

Old English to Middle English to Modern English. Show Old English covering the eighth to the twelfth centuries, Middle English the twelfth to the end of the fifteenth centuries, and Modern English from the sixteenth century to today. Give the following examples of how words have changed:

Old English	**Middle English**	**Modern English**
hēafod	hēved	head
rīdan	rīden	ride
eald	eld	old

2. Use a map to illustrate the influence of Latin on the European languages. Show the extent of the Roman Empire and explain that Latin is the basis for Spanish, French, Portugese, and Italian.

3. Ask the class to speculate about how American Indian words entered the English language.

4. Ask for additional examples of compound words and blends.

5. Discuss *Check It Out.*

6. Assign *Try Your Skill.* Some students may need help in interpreting the information on word origins in their dictionaries. (For answers, see Key at back of book.) After they have mastered this skill, assign *Now Write.* (See Key at back of book.)

After each *Now Write* activity, an additional challenge is offered in the *Write Again* section of the text, beginning on page 193.

Extending the Lesson Explain that cartoons and comic strips often include echoic words. Begin a list of these words on the chalkboard. Have the class search for more examples to add to the list.

Part 2 **Say It Again, Sam** Context: Definition and Restatement
pp. 4-5

Objectives 1. To understand the use of context clues in learning word meanings

2. To use the direct context clues of definition and restatement to learn word meanings

Presenting the Lesson 1. Read aloud and discuss *Here's the Idea.* Highlight the meaning of *context.* Explain that definition and restatement are direct clues because they actually tell what words mean.

2. Discuss *Check It Out.* Help the class to identify the clues used in the sentences.

3. Assign and discuss *Try Your Skill.* Ask students to identify the clues that helped them determine word meaning.

4. Assign *Now Write.* Direct the students to revise their sentences if meanings are not clear.

After each *Now Write* activity, an additional challenge is offered in the *Write Again* section of the text, beginning on page 193.

Extending the Lesson Give the class the following nonsense words.

bertel	hent	spreen
snup	trub	clar
pooler	ambib	noobing

Ask them to choose five of the words and to write a definition for each. Have them use each word in a sentence using definition or restatement in the context.

Part 3 **A Good Example** Using Context Clues: Examples
pp. 6-7

Objective To recognize examples used as context clues

Presenting the Lesson 1. Read aloud and discuss *Here's the Idea.* Clarify the meaning of *example* by asking the class for examples of a food, a color, a flower, and a make of car.

2. Read and discuss *Check It Out.* Emphasize that an example gives a clue to the general meaning of a word, not to the exact meaning.

3. Assign and discuss *Try Your Skill.* Ask students to identify the key words and phrases that signaled the examples.

4. Assign *Now Write.*

After each *Now Write* activity, an additional challenge is offered in the *Write Again* section of the text, beginning on page 193.

Extending the Lesson Direct the students to read in an encyclopedia about the flora and fauna of your particular geographical area. Tell them to list the names of five unusual plants and animals and to use each name in a sentence that has an example in the context.

Part 4 **Like and Unlike** Context Clues: Comparison and Contrast pp. 8-9

Objective To study the use of comparison and contrast as context clues

Presenting the Lesson 1. Read aloud and discuss *Here's the Idea.* Emphasize the difference between comparison and contrast.

2. Read and discuss *Check It Out.* Note that the context clues for *chlorine* and *clove* yield general meanings, while those for *mural* and *prohibited* yield more specific meanings.

3. Assign and discuss *Try Your Skill.* Note that *and other* is a key phrase that signals comparison as a context clue and that *however* is a word that signals contrast.

4. Assign *Now Write.* Encourage students to revise their sentences if readers do not find them clear.

Extending the Lesson Give the students the following sentences. Ask them to learn the meanings of the italicized words from the context clues, then to write two or three sentences that summarize Shel's characteristics.

1. Shel is *rotund,* but Mel is thin.
2. Shel is *garrulous,* while Mel hardly talks at all.
3. Shel is often *deceitful,* but Mel always tells the truth.
4. Shel has an *aversion* to hard word, unlike Mel who enjoys it.
5. Shel was once *incarcerated,* but Mel has never been in prison.

More able students might make up two other characters and write four or five sentences contrasting them. Encourage the students to use their dictionaries to locate unfamiliar words.

Part 5 **Be Precise** Using Synonyms and Antonyms pp. 10-11

Objective To understand the importance of using precise words to express ideas

Presenting the Lesson 1. Read aloud and discuss *Here's the Idea.* Ask the class for additional synonyms for *laugh* and *eat.* Discuss the differences among the meanings. Ask the class for antonyms for *cold, fat,* and *thin.*

2. Read and discuss *Check It Out.* (See Key at back of book.)

Ask students to use the words that were *not* selected in sentences.

3. Assign and discuss *Try Your Skill.* When students understand differences in meaning among words, assign *Now Write.*

Extending the Lesson Introduce the class to *Webster's New Dictionary of Synonyms* or a similar reference book. You might choose the entry for a common word such as *small, bad,* or *make,* duplicate it, and give a copy to each member of the class. You can then discuss the differences among the synonyms for the word or make up a list of specific questions for the students to answer.

Part 6 **Get on Base** Using Words Parts: Base Words pp. 12-13

Objective To learn to recognize base words

Presenting the Lesson 1. Read aloud and discuss *Here's the Idea.* Ask students for additional examples of words that can be built on the base word *move* (*remove, unmoved, moving*).

2. Read and discuss *Check It Out.* (See Key at back of book.) Note that although the final *e* in *adventure* is dropped, the final *e* in *use* is not.

3. Assign and discuss *Try Your Skill.* (See Key at back of book.)

4. Assign *Now Write.*

Extending the Lesson Divide the class into groups of three or four students. Give each group the following list of base words.

mind	turn
honor	rest
hope	sound
perform	law

Set a time limit during which each group must build as many new words as possible using the eight base words.

Part 7 **What's First?** Using Word Parts: Prefixes pp. 14-15

Objective To understand the meanings and use of common prefixes

Presenting the Lesson 1. Read aloud and discuss *Here's the Idea.* Ask the class for additional examples of words that begin with the prefix *un-*. Have students identify any example words that are unfamiliar. Help them to determine the meanings, using the base words and the meanings of the prefixes.

2. Read and discuss *Check It Out.* (See Key at back of book.) Note that *dis* is another prefix meaning "not."

3. Assign and discuss *Try Your Skill.* Work with those students who failed to identify the words that do not have prefixes. (See Key at back of book.)

4. Assign *Now Write.* Remind students that when they look for words beginning with a certain prefix in a dictionary, they will encounter many other words beginning with that prefix.

Extending the Lesson Divide the class into groups of four or five students. Have each group make fifty cards. (Suggest that they cut 3x5 cards in half.) On twenty-five of the cards they should write prefixes introduced in this lesson. On the remaining twenty-five they should write base words. They can then use the cards to play the following game.

1. Each player is dealt six cards. The remaining cards are placed face-down in a pile. One card is turned face-up next to the pile.
2. Each player in turn draws a card from the pile or takes the top card from the face-up pile.
3. The player then must discard one card, face-up.
4. The game ends when a player can arrange the cards in his or her hand to make three complete words, each consisting of a prefix and a base word.

Part 8 **The End** Using Word Parts: Suffixes pp. 16-17

Objective To understand the meanings and use of common suffixes

Presenting the Lesson 1. Read aloud and discuss *Here's the Idea.* Highlight the spelling changes described.

2. Read and discuss *Check It Out.* (See Key at back of book.)

3. Assign and discuss *Try Your Skill.* (See Key at back of book.) Note the spelling change in *religious.* When you are certain that the students understand how suffixes affect the meanings of base words and how the spellings of base words change, assign *Now Write.*

Extending the Lesson 1. Give the students articles from a local newspaper. Ask them to underline words that have suffixes. On the chalkboard, make a four-column chart with these headings: No spelling change, Drop final *e*, Change final *y* to *i*, and Double final consonant. Ask students to put the words they underlined under the right headings.

2. Have each student list seven words that describe himself or herself. Each word should end in one of the suffixes introduced in the lesson.

WRITING SECTION 2

Improving Your Sentences **Pages 19-25**

Objectives

1. To understand what makes a good sentence
2. To learn how to avoid writing sentences with unnecessary repetition of ideas and unsupported opinions
3. To practice the skill of writing succinct sentences

Preparing the Students

Give the class the following groups of words. Ask them to rearrange the words into sentences.

1. the cow moon jumped over purple full the (The purple cow jumped over the full moon.)
2. delicate the spider a web wove determined a (The determined spider wove a delicate web.)

Emphasize the basic differences between the groups of words and the sentences.

1. A sentence expresses a complete thought.
2. A sentence has a subject and a predicate. (You may need to review the definition of each.)
3. A sentence begins with a capital letter and ends with a period, question mark, or exclamation mark.

Part 1 **One of a Kind** Writing Good Sentences pp. 20-21

Objective To understand what makes a good sentence

Presenting the Lesson 1. Read aloud and discuss *Here's the Idea.* Ask students to explain the meanings of the more difficult quotations. Note the wide range of authors represented; for example, Pindar was a Greek poet who lived in the fifth century B.C., while Franklin Roosevelt is a twentieth century American president.

2. Read and discuss *Check It Out.*

3. Assign *Try Your Skill.* Encourage students to revise their sentences until they are satisfied with the results. Ask volunteers to share their sentences with the class. Discuss further improvements.

4. Assign *Now Write.* Remind students to revise their sentences.

After each *Now Write* activity, an additional challenge is offered in the *Write Again* section of the text, beginning on page 193.

Extending the Lesson Select ten familiar aphorisms from *Poor Richard's Almanac* by Benjamin Franklin. Duplicate the aphorisms and provide a copy for each member of the class. Direct students to identify the basic idea of each quotation and to state the same idea in an equally interesting sentence. Have each student select his or her best sentence to share with the class.

Part 2 **Say Something** Avoiding Empty Sentences pp. 22-23

Objective To learn how to avoid writing sentences with unnecessary repetition of ideas and unsupported opinions

Presenting the Lesson 1. Read aloud and discuss *Here's the Idea.* Emphasize that the first type of empty sentence can be improved by simplifying the idea or by adding information, and that the second type can be improved by giving a reason.

2. Read and discuss *Check It Out.* Encourage a variety of answers.

3. Assign and discuss *Try Your Skill.* During the discussion, pinpoint the error in each sentence.

4. Assign *Now Write.* If most of the students write their own empty sentences, have the class work in partners. Each partner can suggest improvements for the other person's sentences.

After each *Now Write* activity, an additional challenge is offered in the *Write Again* section of the text, beginning on page 193.

Extending the Lesson Have each of the students write one-sentence opinions about the following topics. Caution them to include a fact, reason, or example to support each opinion.

the length of the school year	violence among sports' spectators
television	movies
your favorite kind of book	your favorite school subject
clothes	
music	

Be alert for students who may not be able to differentiate between fact and opinion.

Part 3 **Streamlining** Avoiding Padded Sentences pp. 24-25

Objective To practice the skill of writing succinct sentences

Presenting the Lesson 1. Read aloud and discuss *Here's the Idea.* Discuss briefly why padded sentences should be avoided; emphasize that extra words can obscure meaning. Remind the class that the purpose of a sentence is to express an idea.

2. Read and discuss *Check It Out.*

3. Assign *Try Your Skill.* After the class has completed the exercise, discuss the different ways that each sentence was improved.

4. Assign *Now Write.*

Extending the Lesson Have each student draw a cartoon in which two people or animals are responding to the same event or are describing the same object. The situation depicted can be fanciful or realistic. Direct students to write two sentences, one in each speech balloon. One should be a padded sentence; the other should express the same idea without padding.

Exploring Paragraphs

Pages 27-37

Objectives

1. To learn the definition of *paragraph* through the study of representative examples
2. To gain skill in recognizing unity, or the absence of unity, in a paragraph
3. To study the function of a topic sentence in a paragraph
4. To study three ways to develop a paragraph: by using details, by using examples, and by using facts and figures
5. To learn the differences among the three main kinds of paragraphs—narrative, descriptive, and explanatory

Preparing the Students

Discuss the basic purpose of a sentence—to express an idea. Review the capitalization and punctuation of sentences. Introduce the concept that the basic purpose of a paragraph is also to express an idea. However, a paragraph gives more information. Select a paragraph from a social studies or science text or from an encyclopedia. Note the indentation of the first line and the use of complete sentences, correctly punctuated.

Part 1 **Togetherness** Defining a Paragraph pp. 28-29

Objective To learn the definition of *paragraph* through the study of representative examples

Presenting the Lesson 1. Read aloud and discuss *Here's the Idea* and *Check It Out.* Help the class to identify the main idea of each paragraph.

Paragraph 1: the landing of a jet
Paragraph 2: a scene at the lake
Paragraph 3: directions for sprouting beans

Explain, using one of the paragraphs as an example, that all the sentences say something about the main idea. Ask the class to analyze a second paragraph, sentence by sentence.

2. Assign and discuss *Try Your Skill.* Work in a small group with those students who have difficulty with this exercise.

3. Assign *Now Write.*

After each *Now Write* activity, an additional challenge is offered in the *Write Again* section of the text, beginning on page 193.

Extending the Lesson 1. For further practice, have students continue *Now Write,* using a second group of sentences that is not a paragraph.

2. Ask a group of volunteers to begin a poster that will summarize the information on paragraphs presented in Section 3. The poster should be divided into four parts.

A paragraph is . . . (definition)
A paragraph has . . . (describe topic sentence)
A paragraph is developed by . . . (methods of development)
A paragraph can be . . . (describe three main types)

At this point the group should complete only the first part.

Part 2 **All for One** Recognizing Paragraph Unity pp. 30-31

Objective To gain skill in recognizing unity, or the absence of unity, in a paragraph

Presenting the Lesson 1. Read and discuss *Here's the Idea* and *Check It Out.* Emphasize that for a paragraph to have unity, each sentence must relate to the main idea.

2. Assign and discuss *Try Your Skill.* (See Key at back of book.) Work in a small group with those students who were not able to complete this exercise successfully. For the first group of sentences, help students to eliminate those sentences that are not about an elephant's trunk. For the second group, help them to eliminate those sentences that are not about the countries from which immigrants have come.

3. Assign *Now Write. Extending the Lesson* suggests an activity for those students who have difficulty finding a topic.

After each *Now Write* activity, an additional challenge is offered in the *Write Again* section of the text, beginning on page 193.

Extending the Lesson Provide students who have trouble finding a topic with materials at various reading levels. These might include the sports section of a local newspaper; adult magazines such as *Sports Illustrated* and *WomenSports;* children's magazines such as *National Geographic World* and *Pet News;* and books on topics such as Indian crafts, recycling, cooking, and art projects. Help students to compile a list of possible topics and to choose one of them.

Part 3 **What's the Big Idea?** Using a Topic Sentence
pp. 32-33

Objective To study the function of a topic sentence in a paragraph

Presenting the Lesson 1. Read and discuss *Here's the Idea.* Emphasize the importance of the topic sentence. Explain that some writers, especially writers of stories, do not use topic sentences for every paragraph. However, using topic sentences is a good way to learn to structure paragraphs.

2. Read and discuss the paragraph in *Check It Out.* Point out that each sentence relates to the topic sentence.

3. Assign and discuss *Try Your Skill.* (See Key at back of book.) When all of the students can recognize the topic sentence in each group, have them choose two of the groups of sentences and write them as paragraphs. Remind them to put the topic sentence first and to organize the rest of the sentences in logical order.

Extending the Lesson 1. Have students study the sentences they wrote for *Part 2, Now Write.* Tell them to decide on the one idea that is common to all five sentences and to write a topic sentence that expresses that idea.

2. Refer the class to the poster begun in Part 1. Have them add information about the function of a topic sentence.

Part 4 **Show Your Support** Developing a Paragraph
pp. 34-35

Objective To study three ways to develop a paragraph: by using details, by using examples, and by using facts and figures

Presenting the Lesson 1. Read aloud and discuss *Here's the Idea.* Ask the class to identify the details in the first sample paragraph, to explain the example in the second paragraph, and to cite the facts and figures in the third.

2. Read the paragraph in *Check It Out*. Help the class to understand that the main idea stated in the topic sentence is supported by facts and figures. Note that *Scientific American* is the source of the paragraph.

3. Assign and discuss *Try Your Skill*.

4. Assign *Now Write*.

Extending the Lesson 1. Give the class the following topic sentences, either orally or in writing. Ask students to think about the types of information that might be included in each paragraph and to decide which method of development is best suited to the topic.

> Scat the Cat is smarter than most people.
> A hardware store has something for everyone.
> The community of Roselawn includes people of all ages, incomes, and races.
> Dawn is a gentle time.
> The Museum of Natural History is famous for its exhibits of Midwestern wildlife.

2. Refer the class to the poster begun in Part 1. Have them add information about ways to develop a paragraph.

Part 5 **Brand Names** Recognizing Three Kinds of Paragraphs

pp. 36-37

Objective To learn the differences among the three main kinds of paragraphs—narrative, descriptive, and explanatory

Presenting the Lesson 1. Read and discuss *Here's the Idea*. Emphasize that narrative paragraphs and the *how* kind of explanatory paragraph are written in time sequence.

2. Read and discuss the paragraph in *Check It Out*.

3. Assign and discuss *Try Your Skill*. Emphasize the importance of details in each type of paragraph, using the four sample paragraphs in this lesson.

4. Assign *Now Write*. To help students decide which type of paragraph they would use, have each student state the purpose of his or her paragraph in one sentence; for example: I want to explain how to select a good campsite.

Extending the Lesson 1. Divide a duplicating master into three columns headed Narrative, Descriptive, and Explanatory. Record the topics that the students selected for *Parts 3, 4,* and *5, Now Write* in the proper columns. Discuss with the class the variety of subjects represented and the types of topics that are listed in each column.

2. Refer to the poster begun in Part 1. Complete it by adding information about the different kinds of paragraphs.

WRITING SECTION 4

Writing a Paragraph

Pages 39-47

Objectives

1. To understand and to apply the process of narrowing a topic
2. To learn to write direct, interesting topic sentences
3. To learn to develop paragraphs by using details, examples, or facts and figures
4. To gain skill in writing a paragraph ending that sums up the main idea in an interesting way

Preparing the Students

Refer once again to the poster developed throughout Section 3. Highlight the main points and explain that in Section 4, the students will learn to apply what they have learned about paragraphs.

Part 1 The Straight and Narrow Narrowing a Topic

pp. 40-41

Objective To understand and to apply the process of narrowing a topic

Presenting the Lesson 1. Read aloud and discuss *Here's the Idea.* Contrast the meanings of *general* and *specific* topics. Use the following examples:

General	Specific
food	how to boil an egg
	how to recognize a ripe cantaloupe
school	the first day of school
entertainment	the last Fourth of July parade

Emphasize that the six questions can be used to narrow a general topic. Note that the answers to the questions are incorporated into the paragraph.

2. Discuss *Check It Out.* Note that four of the six answers are included in the narrow topic.

3. Assign and discuss *Try Your Skill.* Evaluate whether each narrowed topic can be covered in one paragraph. Point out that many different specific topics can be drawn from one general topic.

4. Assign *Now Write.* Work with those students who need further help in narrowing their topics.

Extending the Lesson Select three one-paragraph "filler" articles from a local newspaper. Duplicate them and give a copy to each student. Have students answer the questions who? what? when? where? how? and why? for each article.

Part 2 **Direct Contact** Writing a Topic Sentence pp. 42-43

Objective To learn to write direct, interesting topic sentences

Presenting the Lesson 1. Read aloud and discuss *Here's the Idea.* Emphasize the twofold purpose of a topic sentence: to state the main idea of a paragraph and to stimulate interest in the paragraph.

2. Read and discuss *Check It Out.*

3. Assign *Try Your Skill.* Encourage students to try different approaches to each sentence before deciding on a final version. Remind them to write humorous sentences only for humorous topics. After the class has completed this exercise, compare the new versions of each sentence. Each student should be able to write a direct sentence, without unnecessary words. However, many students will not be able to write a humorous sentence at this point.

4. Assign *Now Write.*

Extending the Lesson Direct each student to find one example of an opening sentence that includes humor, rhyme, or an unusual twist. Suggest magazines and newspaper features as good sources. For some groups of students, you may need to provide the sources. Set aside bulletin board space to display the examples.

Part 3 **The Main Road** Developing a Paragraph pp. 44-45

Objective To learn to develop paragraphs by using details, examples, or facts and figures

Presenting the Lesson 1. Read aloud and discuss *Here's the Idea.* If the class needs a more detailed review of the three types of paragraph development, refer to the lesson *Show Your Support* (pages 34-35) and read a sample of each type.

2. Read and discuss *Check It Out.* Ask students to identify the details in the paragraph.

3. Assign and discuss *Try Your Skill.* Ask several students to explain their choices.

4. Assign *Now Write.* Work in a small group with those students who are not sure of what method to use. Ask each student to describe what he or she wants to say in the paragraph. Ask the rest of the group to suggest a possible method (or methods) of development.

Extending the Lesson For *Now Write,* each student selected one topic sentence. Direct students to decide the best method of development for the topic sentence they did *not* choose.

Part 4 **A Stop Sign** Ending a Paragraph pp. 46-47

Objective To gain skill in writing a paragraph ending that sums up the main idea in an interesting way

Presenting the Lesson 1. Read aloud and discuss *Here's the Idea.*

2. Read and discuss *Check It Out.* Point out that the ending reinforces the idea of mystery introduced in the topic sentence.

3. Assign *Try Your Skill.* Remind the class to eliminate each poor ending sentence before adding the new ending.

4. Assign *Now Write.* Before students write their paragraphs in final form, suggest that they do exercise 1 in *Extending the Lesson.*

Extending the Lesson 1. Tell the students to exchange their paragraphs with a partner and to check each other's paragraphs for the following:

Completeness of sentences
Mechanics such as capitalization and punctuation of sentences and indentation of the paragraph
Spelling
A direct, interesting topic sentence
Sentences that develop the idea in the topic sentence
An ending that sums up the main idea

Have each student write any suggestions for improvement on a separate sheet of paper.

2. Introduce the idea of putting out a magazine-type collection of the students' writing. Explain that periodically you will ask for samples of their writing to save for the collection. Encourage students to turn in copies of their completed paragraphs.

WRITING SECTION 5

A Writer's Choices

Pages 49-61

Objectives

1. To review the literary meaning of *point of view*
2. To study and use first-person point of view
3. To apply an understanding of third-person point of view
4. To understand the importance of accuracy in writing about real people, places, events, or things
5. To realize the importance of details in imaginary writing
6. To master the use of specific verbs to create mood
7. To study and to practice writing interesting titles

Preparing the Students

Introduce the concept of point of view by doing the following:

1. Divide the class in half. Ask the first group of students to close their eyes and to imagine themselves walking toward an eighty-story office building. (Some classes might need the help of a picture.) Ask them to contribute phrases that describe what they see as they look up at the building. List these on the chalkboard.

2. Next, ask the other half of the class to imagine themselves on the top floor of the same building. Have them describe what they see as they look down. Record these phrases on the chalkboard.

3. Discuss point of view as the way a person looks at something.

Part 1 **Who, Me?** Using a Personal Point of View pp. 50-51

Objectives 1. To review the literary meaning of *point of view*
2. To study and use first-person point of view

Presenting the Lesson 1. Read aloud and discuss *Here's the Idea.* Give the class the following sentences as examples of first-person point of view:

> I am a very small fish in a very big pond. (imaginary writing)
>
> I am a good volley ball player. (writing based on real life)

Emphasize the use of *I.*

2. Read and discuss the sample paragraph in *Check It Out.*

3. Assign *Try Your Skill.* Remind the class that in the first-person point of view, the narrator (or *I*) can't tell what anyone else is thinking or feeling.

4. Assign *Now Write.*

Extending the Lesson Read a selection or two from the book *Ben and Me* by Robert Lawson. (It is a story about a mouse who "helps" Benjamin Franklin with his important inventions, written from the point of view of the mouse.) Discuss the author's use of point of view. Ask students to find other examples of fiction written in first-person point of view.

Part 2 **Out of Sight** Using an Outsider's Point of View
pp. 52-53

Objective To apply an understanding of third-person point of view

Presenting the Lesson 1. Read aloud and discuss *Here's the Idea.* Compare and contrast first-person and third-person point of view.

2. Read and discuss *Check It Out.* Ask the class to reread the paragraph, substituting first the pronoun *he* (with appropriate name changes for Ruth and Diana), then the pronoun *they* (with the addition of two characters).

3. Assign *Try Your Skill.* Remind the class that in third-person point of view, what the characters are thinking and feeling isn't revealed.

4. Assign *Now Write.*

Extending the Lesson On the chalkboard, list the names of public places where the students can spend time observing activity. These might include a library, a bus or train station, a park, a gas station, a grocery or department store, and a busy intersection. Ask the class for additional suggestions. Then assign volunteers to cover each place. After a short period of observation (10-15 minutes), each student should write five sentences about what he or she saw and heard. Discuss the observations in class.

Part 3 **To Tell the Truth** Writing About What Is Real
pp. 54-55

Objective To understand the importance of accuracy in writing about real people, places, events, or things

Presenting the Lesson 1. Read aloud and discuss *Here's the Idea.* Emphasize the importance of accuracy. Note the location of the various reference books named.

2. Read and discuss the sample paragraph in *Check It Out.*

3. Assign *Try Your Skill.* Direct the students to use reference books to find, as well as to check, information.

4. Assign *Now Write.* On the chalkboard list the steps that the students will follow.

Choose a topic.
Narrow the topic.
List details.
Decide on the kind of paragraph.
Decide on first-person or third-person point of view.
Write a first draft.
Revise.
Make a final copy.

Work with the students who have difficulty.

Extending the Lesson 1. Have each student find eight little-known or unusual facts about people, animals, and places. Encourage the class to use encyclopedias, books about animals, the *Guinness Book of World Records*, and *Ripley's Believe It Or Not.*

2. Make it a class project to learn interesting facts about the city in which you live.

3. Some students may want to contribute the paragraphs they wrote for *Now Write* to the class magazine.

Part 4 **Mind over Matter** Writing About What Is Imaginary pp. 56-57

Objective To realize the importance of details in imaginary writing

Presenting the Lesson 1. Read aloud and discuss *Here's the Idea.* Explain that some imaginary writings are about things that could happen in real life; for example, stories about children growing up. Others, though, are about things that couldn't possibly happen; for example, stories about animals who act like human beings.

2. Read and discuss the sample paragraph in *Check It Out.*

3. Assign *Try Your Skill.* Provide time for the students to share their sentences. Discuss the specific details included in each sentence. Identify those students who need further help in using details.

4. Assign *Now Write.* Work with those students who need help in using details; use Exercise 1 in *Extending the Lesson.*

Extending the Lesson 1. Tell each student to divide a sheet of paper into five columns and to head the columns *sight, hearing, taste, touch,* and *smell.* Have the students list words related to each sense; for example, they might write *rough* under *touch.* Encourage them to use their dictionaries.

2. Some students may want to contribute the paragraphs they wrote for *Now Write* to the class magazine.

Part 5 **First Choice** Choosing the Right Verb pp. 58-59

Objective To master the use of specific verbs to create mood

Presenting the Lesson 1. Read aloud and discuss *Here's the Idea.* Review the difference between an action verb and a linking verb. Ask volunteers to act out the variations in meaning among the synonyms for *walk.*

2. Review the use of a thesaurus or dictionary of synonyms.

3. Read and discuss the sample paragraph in *Check It Out.* Help students understand how the overall mood of excitement and urgency is created.

4. Assign *Try Your Skill.* Encourage students to use a dictionary or thesaurus to find substitutes for *said.*

5. Assign *Now Write.*

Extending the Lesson Have the students list substitutes for the verb *talk.* Ask them to write one sentence for each of the following moods: excited, terrified, dejected, angry, determined, and hesitant. Each sentence should contain one of the substitute verbs. For some classes, you may need to discuss briefly the probable feelings, actions, and thoughts connected with each mood.

Part 6 **The Name Game** Writing a Title That Works pp. 60-61

Objective To study and to practice writing interesting titles

Presenting the Lesson 1. Read aloud and discuss *Here's the Idea.* Highlight the twofold purpose of a title:

To catch a reader's attention
To indicate a main idea

2. Discuss the titles in *Check It Out.* Ask students for additional examples.

3. Assign *Try Your Skill.* Encourage students to try several different titles for each topic before deciding on two.

4. Assign *Now Write.* After students have completed this exercise, ask volunteers to share their titles with the class. Discuss how well each fulfills the purpose of a title.

Extending the Lesson Discuss the way titles have been used in this book. Ask students to identify those that are variations on other titles and on familiar expressions (Alive and Well/Jacques Brel Is Alive and Well and Living in Paris; Say It Again, Sam/Play It Again, Sam; All for One/All for One and One for All).

The Process of Writing

Pages 63-67

Objectives

1. To understand the choices involved in planning a piece of writing
2. To learn to write a first draft
3. To study the process of revising, rewriting, and proofreading

Preparing the Students

Divide the chalkboard into three columns headed *Before, During,* and *After.* Review with the class the Writer's Choices presented in Section 5. Point out that most of these choices must be made before any writing is done and, therefore, are *before* activities. Explain that in this section, the students will study the entire writing process.

Presenting the Lesson 1. Read and discuss *Before You Write.* List the following steps on the chalkboard under *Before:*

Choose a topic.
Narrow the topic.
Choose a point of view.
List details.

2. Discuss the sample pre-writing notes. Point out that the writer listed several topics (none of which needed narrowing), chose the county fair, listed details, decided on a descriptive paragraph and the first-person point of view, and noted the desired mood. Add the following to the chalkboard list:

Decide on the kind of paragraph. (Insert after "Narrow the topic.")
Note mood. (Add after "List details.")

3. Discuss *When You Write.* Emphasize that the product of this step is a rough draft. On the chalkboard, under *During,* write the following:

Write a rough draft.
Ignore writing, organization, spelling, and punctuation.

4. Read the sample rough draft.

5. Read and discuss *After You Write*. As each main step is introduced, write it on the chalkboard under *After*. Include the following:

Reread for content.
Review for clear expression of ideas.
Check for organization.
Check words for appropriateness.
Check spelling, capitalization, and punctuation.
Write a title, if necessary.
Rewrite.
Proofread.

6. Compare the rough draft and the revised copy of the sample paragraph. Note the addition of specific details and of phrases that indicate spacial relationships, and the substitution of strong verbs for weak ones.

Extending the Lesson Ask a group of three or four students to transfer the information on the chalkboard chart to a large sheet of poster paper or to a bulletin board. Use the chart for reference.

WRITING SECTION 7

The Narrative Paragraph

Pages 69-75

Objectives

1. To review the meaning of *narrative paragraph*
2. To apply an understanding of chronological order as a major characteristic of narrative writing
3. To gain skill in using transitions to indicate chronological order
4. To learn to use details in developing narrative paragraphs

Preparing the Students

Read aloud a sample narrative paragraph from Section 3, Part 5. Review the main characteristics of a narrative paragraph:

It tells a story.
It is written in chronological order.

Part 1 **Then What Happened?** Using Chronological Order
pp. 70-71

Objectives 1. To review the meaning of *narrative paragraph*
2. To apply an understanding of chronological order as a major characteristic of narrative writing

Presenting the Lesson 1. Read aloud and discuss *Here's the Idea.* Emphasize that a narrative paragraph relates events in the order in which they happened. Introduce the terms *time order* and *time sequence* as synonyms for *chronological order.* Explain that chronological order is a *natural* or *logical* order for a narrative paragraph. Ask students to identify the events described in the sample paragraph. Point out that although the paragraph does not begin with a topic sentence, it does open with a strong, lively sentence that draws the reader immediately into the paragraph.
2. Read and discuss *Check It Out.*
3. Assign and discuss *Try Your Skill.* Work in a small group with those students who have difficulty with this exercise.
4. Assign *Now Write.* Refer the class to the Process of Writing chart.

Extending the Lesson Divide the class into partners. Have each pair choose a television program that has a strong story line. After watching the program, each student should write five or six sentences that state the main events of the plot in chronological order. Direct the partners to compare their sentences and to revise them, if necessary. Tell them to save their sentences for use after the next lesson.

Part 2 **How Time Flies!** Using Transitions in a Narrative
pp. 72-73

Objective To gain skill in using transitions to indicate chronological order

Presenting the Lesson 1. Ask several volunteers to describe what they did after school the previous day. Point out the automatic use of transitions.

2. Read aloud and discuss *Here's the Idea.* Emphasize the function of transitions: to show chronological order.

3. Read and discuss *Check It Out.* Explain that a phrase such as "I was awakened" indicates the passage of time, although it is not strictly a transition.

4. Assign *Try Your Skill.* Remind the students to choose a variety of transitions. Ask volunteers to share their rewritten paragraphs with the class. Discuss the different choices of transitions.

5. Assign *Now Write.* Refer students to the Process of Writing chart.

Extending the Lesson Ask students to take out the sentences they wrote for *Part 1, Extending the Lesson.* Have them combine the sentences into one-paragraph summaries of the television programs. Remind them to use a variety of transitions.

Part 3 **In Detail** Developing a Narrative Paragraph pp. 74-75

Objective To learn to use details in developing narrative paragraphs

Presenting the Lesson 1. Read aloud and discuss *Here's the Idea.* Emphasize that the details generated by the six questions are incorporated into the description of what happened.

2. Read and discuss the sample paragraph in *Check It Out.* Ask students to identify the details and the transitional words and phrases.

3. Assign *Try Your Skill.* Remind the students to incorporate the details into their lists of events. After the students have completed this exercise successfully, assign *Now Write.*

Extending the Lesson 1. Have each student interview a relative or a student in another class about that person's most memorable goodbye. Remind the class to use the six questions to elicit details from the person. After the interviews are completed, have the students write narrative paragraphs that include the details.

2. Each student has written several paragraphs for Section 7. Encourage the class to contribute paragraphs to the class magazine.

The Descriptive Paragraph

Pages 77-85

Objectives

1. To learn to include sensory details in descriptive paragraphs
2. To gain skill in choosing adjectives that contribute to a desired mood
3. To study ways to organize descriptive paragraphs in spatial order
4. To practice using transitional words and phrases to show spatial order

Preparing the Students

Select travel brochures that advertise several different places. Read the place descriptions to the students. Ask them to form mental pictures as they listen. Review the definition of *descriptive paragraph* (a picture in words).

Part 1 **You Are There** Using Your Senses in Description

pp. 78-79

Objective To learn to include sensory details in descriptive paragraphs

Presenting the Lesson 1. Read aloud and discuss *Here's the Idea.* Emphasize the importance of details if a writer is to share an experience with a reader. Explain that details can be colorful adjectives or adverbs, specific nouns, strong verbs, or descriptive phrases. Ask students to identify the details in the sample paragraph and to name the sense to which each detail appeals.

2. Read and discuss *Check It Out.*

3. Assign *Try Your Skill.* Remind students to make their details specific.

4. Assign *Now Write.* Some students may need help in organizing their details, as this skill is not introduced until Part 3.

Extending the Lesson Have students select one of the two topics they chose for *Try Your Skill* and write a paragraph that incorporates the sensory details they listed. Provide time for the students who wrote about the same topic to compare the sensory details they used.

Part 2 The Right Mood Using Adjectives To Create Mood pp. 80-81

Objective To gain skill in choosing adjectives that contribute to a desired mood

Presenting the Lesson 1. Read aloud and discuss *Here's the Idea.* Explain that many words suggest meanings beyond their literal meanings. These extended meanings are called the *connotation* of words. Give the class these additional examples of positive and negative connotations:

Positive	Negative
thin	skinny
bright	garish
fitted	tight
reserved	stiff

2. Read and discuss *Check It Out.*

3. Assign and discuss *Try Your Skill.* Work with those students who have difficulty maintaining consistency among their adjectives. After students have completed *Try Your Skill* successfully, assign *Now Write.*

Extending the Lesson Explain to the class that restaurant menus often contain many adjectives with positive connotations; for example, *tangy* barbeque sauce or a *frosty* mug of root beer. Divide the class into groups of four or five students. Direct each group to create a sample menu that describes at least three foods in each of the following categories: eggs, meat, fish, fowl, vegetables, salads, and beverages.

Part 3 Look Around Using Spatial Order pp. 82-83

Objective To study ways to organize descriptive paragraphs in spatial order

Presenting the Lesson 1. Read aloud and discuss *Here's the Idea.* Compare spatial order with chronological order. Note that the old apartment building is described from top to bottom.

2. Read and discuss the sample paragraph in *Check It Out.* Note the top to bottom order. Ask students to identify the details in the paragraph.

3. Assign *Try Your Skill.* For further practice, see *Extending the Lesson.*

4. Assign *Now Write.* Remind students that before revising their paragraphs, they should trade papers with a partner and try to draw a picture from each other's description.

Extending the Lesson Display in the classroom some pictures of various types of environments; for example: jungle, Arctic, underwater, and desert. Make sure that each picture has a strong main focus. Direct each student to choose one of the pictures and to follow the directions for *Try Your Skill.* Tell them to save their lists for use in the next lesson.

Part 4 **A Place for Everything** Using Transitions in a Description

pp. 84-85

Objective To practice using transitional words and phrases to show spatial order

Presenting the Lesson 1. Read aloud and discuss *Here's the Idea.* Ask students for sentences that show spatial relationships among objects in the classroom; note the transitional words. Ask the class to identify the transitions in the sample paragraph. Besides the word *inside,* which is on the list, the paragraph includes *atop, outer,* and *inner.* You might point out that the paragraph is a combination of a narration (It tells about something that happened) and a description (It paints a picture of the orange).

2. Read and discuss *Check It Out.* Note the spatial order followed by the writer.

3. Assign *Try Your Skill.* Work in a small group with those students who have difficulty understanding and indicating spatial relationships.

4. Assign *Now Write.* Remind the students who choose to describe a person that usually a writer begins at the top and proceeds downward.

Extending the Lesson 1. Ask students to take out the lists that they developed for *Part 3, Extending the Lesson.* Display the same pictures once again. Direct the class to complete their paragraphs by doing the following:

Add transitional words and phrases to show spatial order.
List sensory details.
Write a first draft.
Revise and rewrite.

2. Encourage students to contribute the paragraphs they wrote for Section 8 to the class magazine.

WRITING SECTION 9

The Explanatory Paragraph

Telling *How* **Pages 88-93**

Objectives

1. To learn to write a paragraph that explains how to do or to make something
2. To understand the importance of giving directions in an organized, step-by-step way
3. To gain skill in using transitions to show step-by-step order

Preparing the Students

Review the two kinds of paragraphs that students have learned to write. Emphasize that in a narrative paragraph a writer shares an experience, or something that happened, with a reader; in a descriptive paragraph a writer shares a sense impression of a person, place, or object. Review the meaning of *explanatory paragraph.* Explain that in an explanatory *how* paragraph a writer shares his or her knowledge and skills.

Part 1 **Here's How!** Planning an Explanation pp. 88-89

Objective To learn to write a paragraph that explains how to do or to make something

Presenting the Lesson 1. Read aloud and discuss *Here's the Idea.* Emphasize the importance of selecting a simple process. This eliminates the need for narrowing the topic.

2. Read and discuss the sample paragraph in *Check It Out.* To emphasize the specificity of the directions, ask a volunteer to demonstrate the process of repotting as it is explained in the paragraph.

3. Assign *Try Your Skill.* Compare an actual recipe for beef stew with the one given. For further examples of recipes written by young children, read selections from the book *Smashed Potatoes* by Jane G. Martel.

4. Assign *Now Write.*

Extending the Lesson With the class, decide on three or four simple-to-make foods; for example, a root beer float, toasted marshmallows, hot dogs, popcorn, and lemonade. Have each student choose one and write a recipe for it. Then have the student ask a five or six-year-old child to explain how to make the same food and write the child's answer. Display the most interesting results on a bulletin board opposite the actual recipes for the foods.

Part 2 **Get in Step** Using Step-by-Step Order pp. 90-91

Objective To understand the importance of giving directions in an organized, step-by-step way

Presenting the Lesson 1. Read aloud and discuss *Here's the Idea.*

2. Read and discuss the sample paragraph in *Check It Out.* Point out that the paragraph begins with a topic sentence that states the main idea. Ask the class to identify the information that has been added to the basic steps.

3. Assign *Try Your Skill.* Caution the students to choose simple games. Work in a small group with those students whose directions were not clear.

4. Assign *Now Write.*

Extending the Lesson Tell the students to imagine that they are designers of cereal boxes. They have been asked to include a game, puzzle, magic trick, or simple science experiment in their designs. Have each student choose one and write a paragraph that explains the process in step-by-step order.

Part 3 **In Order** Using Transitions in an Explanation

pp. 92-93

Objective To gain skill in using transitions to show step-by-step order

Presenting the Lesson 1. Read aloud and discuss *Here's the Idea*. Tell students to take the paragraphs they wrote for *Part 2, Now Write* out of their folders. Ask them to identify the transitions they used to show order.

2. Read and discuss *Check It Out*. Note the opening topic sentence.

3. Assign *Try Your Skill*. Remind students that they can use transitions other than those listed in *Here's the Idea*.

4. Assign *Now Write*. For an activity to help those students who have difficulty finding a topic, see *Extending the Lesson*.

Extending the Lesson 1. For those students who have difficulty choosing a topic for *Now Write*, do one or more of the following:

Provide students with several cookbooks. Have them turn to the section on vegetables. Ask them to identify one that is unfamiliar to them, then read about how to prepare it.

Have students visit the produce section of a local supermarket. Tell them to buy one fruit or vegetable that they have never tasted before. Have them ask an adult for directions on how to prepare it.

Tell students to imagine that they have a large ball, a rope, and a piece of chalk. Ask them to invent a game to be played by six people.

Have students ask a pet owner, the owner of a pet shop, or the director of a dog obedience school for information on how to feed a dog, cat, bird, or fish, or on how to teach one of these pets a trick.

2. Encourage students to contribute paragraphs written for Section 9 to the class magazine.

The Explanatory Paragraph

Telling *Why*

Pages 95-101

Objectives

1. To learn to express an opinion in writing
2. To understand the necessity for supporting opinions with convincing reasons, organized from the least important to the most important
3. To gain skill in using transitions to show the order of importance among reasons
4. To develop explanatory *why* paragraphs with effective opening and concluding sentences

Preparing the Students

Review the difference between *fact* and *opinion*, using the following sentences:

1. Fact: A peach is a kind of fruit.
   Opinion: Peaches are delicious.
2. Fact: The Hot Dog Shack serves twelve kinds of hot dogs.
   Opinion: The Hot Dog Shack serves delicious hot dogs.
3. Fact: Marla won the city swimming championship last year.
   Opinion: The city should build a new swimming pool in our neighborhood.

Part 1 State Your Case Stating an Opinion

pp. 96-97

Objective To learn to express an opinion in writing

Presenting the Lesson 1. Read aloud and discuss *Here's the Idea*. Ask students for their opinions on the subjects named in paragraph 1.

2. Read and discuss *Check It Out*. Help the class to identify the opinion that is explained in the paragraph. Point out that it is expressed in the topic sentence.

3. Assign and discuss *Try Your Skill*.

4. Assign *Now Write*. Point out that students are asked to list reasons to support their opinions.

Extending the Lesson Select a short editorial and several letters to the editor from a local newspaper. Duplicate them and give a copy to each member of the class. Direct students to write the opinion expressed in each selection in their own words.

Part 2 **Be Reasonable** Developing an Opinion pp. 98-99

Objective To understand the necessity for supporting opinions with convincing reasons, organized from the least important to the most important

Presenting the Lesson 1. Read aloud and discuss *Here's the Idea*.

2. Read and discuss the sample paragraph in *Check It Out*. Ask the class to identify the opinion expressed in the topic sentence. On the chalkboard, list the reasons given to support the opinion.

3. Assign *Try Your Skill*. Encourage students to read about the benefits of exercise before attempting to develop the reasons for number 1.

4. Assign *Now Write*. Work in a small group with those students who have difficulty completing the exercise.

Extending the Lesson Set up a classroom suggestion box. Encourage students to suggest activities and changes in class organization. The suggestions should be written in the form of opinions supported by reasons.

Part 3 **The Defense Rests** Using Transitions pp. 100-101

Objectives 1. To gain skill in using transitions to show the order of importance among reasons

2. To develop explanatory *why* paragraphs with effective opening and concluding sentences

Presenting the Lesson 1. Read aloud and discuss *Here's the Idea.* Emphasize the following:

An explanatory *why* paragraph should begin with a strong statement of opinion.
It should be developed with convincing reasons, organized from the weakest to the strongest.
It should end with a summary of the argument.

2. Study the three-step process presented in *Check It Out.* Read and discuss the completed paragraph.

3. Assign *Try Your Skill.* After students have arranged the reasons in order, have them expand the reasons by adding details and transitions.

4. Assign *Now Write.*

Extending the Lesson 1. Divide the class into partners. Direct each pair to select a product that is made by at least two different companies; for example, soap, baseball gloves, and frozen pizzas. Each of the partners should select different brands and write a paragraph that explains why theirs is the best brand. Provide time for the partners to read their paragraphs to the class. After each presentation, ask the class to decide which brand they would buy, based on the reasons given.

2. Encourage students to contribute paragraphs written for Section 10 to the class magazine.

WRITING SECTION 11

The Explanatory Paragraph

Telling *What*

Pages 103-107

Objectives

1. To understand that a complete definition includes both general and specific characteristics
2. To learn to state and develop a definition in paragraph form

Preparing the Students

Ask students what comes to mind when they hear the word *definition.* Most will probably say the dictionary. Explain that in this section they will study another type of definition—a definition in paragraph form.

Part 1 **What Is It?** Stating a Definition pp. 104-105

Objective To understand that a complete definition includes both general and specific characteristics

Presenting the Lesson 1. Read aloud and discuss *Here's the Idea.* Point out that writing a specific definition is similar to the process followed when narrowing a topic. Emphasize that the topic sentence states the definition, while the rest of the sentences add specific details.

2. Read and discuss the sample paragraph in *Check It Out.* Ask students to name the general class and specific characteristics that are included in the topic sentence.

3. Assign *Try Your Skill.* Remind the class that the directions call for a one-sentence definition for each object.

4. Assign *Now Write.* Note that for this exercise, the students must write a complete paragraph.

Extending the Lesson Ask volunteers to read the paragraphs they wrote for *Now Write* to the class. Have them substitute a nonsense word such as *blep* for the names of the objects. Ask the rest of the class to identify the object being defined.

Part 2 **Be Particular** Developing a Definition pp. 106-107

Objective To learn to state and develop a definition in paragraph form

Presenting the Lesson 1. Read aloud and discuss *Here's the Idea.* Review the two basic components of a definition (general class, specific characteristics).

2. Read and discuss the sample paragraph in *Check It Out*. Ask the class to read the definition and to identify the general class and specific characteristics included. Point out that the definition is stated in the topic sentence.

3. Assign *Try Your Skill*. Remind the class that a definition is stated in one sentence.

4. Assign *Now Write*. Encourage students to use reference books as necessary.

Extending the Lesson 1. Select three short entries from an encyclopedia. Duplicate them and give a copy to each member of the class. Direct the class to do the following for each entry:

Underline the definition.
Circle the general class of the subject.
Draw a box around the specific characteristics.
Draw two lines under each fact and figure used to develop the definition.

2. Ask the class to contribute paragraphs written for Section 11 to the class magazine. At this point, you most likely have enough selections for a first issue. Appoint a volunteer committee to arrange the paragraphs. They can organize them by type or by content. Duplicate the magazine and distribute a copy to each member of the class.

WRITING SECTION 12

Exploring Compositions

Pages 109-115

Objectives

1. To understand the identifying characteristics of a composition
2. To study the three parts of a composition—introduction, body, and conclusion
3. To learn to recognize narrative, descriptive, and explanatory compositions

Preparing the Students

On the chalkboard, write the following:

composition
paragraph
sentence
word
letter

Discuss the progression from letter to composition, pointing out that each level is built on and goes beyond the one before it; for example, a word is made up of letters arranged so that they communicate a meaning.

Part 1 **Take a Look** Defining a Composition pp. 110-111

Objective To understand the identifying characteristics of a composition

Presenting the Lesson 1. Read aloud and discuss *Here's the Idea.* Highlight the definition of a composition.

2. Read the sample paragraph in *Check It Out.* Ask students to identify the five paragraphs of the composition. Note that each paragraph begins with a topic sentence.

3. Assign and discuss *Try Your Skill.* There may be some variations among the answers, dependingon the students' ideas about probable content.

4. Assign *Now Write.*

Extending the Lesson Refer theclass back to the topics in *Try Your Skill.* Have students broaden the paragraph topics so that the topics could also be the subjects of compositions.

Part 2 **Triple Play** Developing a Composition pp. 112-113

Objective To study the three parts of a composition—introduction, body, and conclusion

Presenting the Lesson 1. Read aloud and discuss *Here's the Idea.*

2. Read and discuss the sample composition in *Check It Out.* Ask the class the following questions:

Does the introduction tell what the composition will be about? What is the main idea?
What details are included in the body?
Is the conclusion a summary, or ending signal?

3. Assign *Try Your Skill.* Ask the class to speculate about what happened before the action described in the paragraph and about what might have happened after.

4. Assign *Now Write.*

Extending the Lesson With the class, begin to plan a two-part bulletin board. The upper portion will summarize the characteristics of all compositions; the lower portion will define the three kinds of compositions and provide space for display of examples.

Part 3 **Name Tags** Recognizing Three Kinds of Compositions

pp. 114-115

Objective To learn to recognize narrative, explanatory, and descriptive kinds of compositions

Presenting the Lesson 1. Read aloud and discuss *Here's the Idea.* Give the class examples of specific topics that might be developed into each type of composition.

2. Read and discuss the sample paragraph in *Check It Out.* Ask the class to identify the introduction, body, and conclusion. Help students to understand that the composition states an opinion and gives reasons to support it; therefore, it is an explanatory *why* composition.

3. Assign and discuss *Try Your Skill.*

4. Assign *Now Write.*

Extending the Lesson 1. Prepare a worksheet on which is listed at least ten of the topics written by the students for *Now Write.* Direct the class to identify which method of development is appropriate for each topic.

2. Appoint a group to complete the bulletin board. As the students write compositions for the following sections, select examples to display on the board.

The Narrative Composition

Pages 117-133

Objectives

1. To study the steps involved in planning a narrative composition based on real life or imaginary experiences
2. To practice recognizing, selecting, and using an appropriate point of view
3. To learn to write an effective introduction to a narrative composition
4. To understand the importance of details to the development of plot and conflict
5. To gain skill in using dialogue to further plot development
6. To gain skill in using dialogue to reveal character
7. To recognize and use transitions within and between the paragraphs of a narrative composition
8. To learn to complete a narrative composition with a strong conclusion and an interesting title

Preparing the Students

Review with the class the definition of *composition* (a group of paragraphs dealing with one idea). Read "The Block Party," the sample composition in Section 12, Part 1. Review the meaning of *narrative composition* using this example.

Part 1 True or False? Planning a Narrative Composition

pp. 118-119

Objective To study the steps involved in planning a narrative composition based on real life or imaginary experiences

Presenting the Lesson 1. Read aloud and discuss *Here's the Idea.* Refer to the *before* section of the Process of Writing chart developed for Section 6. Emphasize the three main elements.

Characters (whoever takes part in a story)
Setting (where the action takes place)
Plot (what happens)

Ask the class for an example of each, using a book or story familiar to most of the class.

2. Read and discuss *Check It Out*. Ask the class to answer the questions who? what? when? where? how? and why? about the topic. Ask a volunteer to summarize the plot in his or her own words.

3. Assign and discuss *Try Your Skill*. Remind the students to use the six questions.

4. Assign *Now Write*. Some students may need help in choosing a topic. Refer them to the ideas in *Try Your Skill*. Remind them to choose a topic other than the one they already worked on.

Extending the Lesson Duplicate a short fable, myth, folk tale, or biographical incident and give a copy to each member of the class. Have each student identify whether it is a true account or a story, name the characters, describe the setting (if possible), and list the main events of the plot.

Part 2 What Do You Know? Using Point of View

pp. 120-121

Objective To practice recognizing, selecting, and using an appropriate point of view

Presenting the Lesson 1. Read aloud and discuss *Here's the Idea*. Emphasize the differences among the three points of view.

2. Read and discuss the sample paragraphs in *Check It Out*. Help students identify paragraph 1 as first-person point of view and paragraph 2 as omniscient point of view.

3. Assign and discuss *Try Your Skill*.

4. Assign *Now Write*.

Extending the Lesson Divide the class into three groups. Direct the students in group 1 to rewrite the sentences in *Try Your Skill* as a paragraph with first-person point of view. Direct group 2 to do the same thing using third–person point of view. Direct group 3 to use omniscient point of view. Select one paragraph from each group and discuss the differences.

Part 3 **Best Foot Forward** Writing an Introduction
pp. 122-123

Objective To learn to write an effective introduction to a narrative composition

Presenting the Lesson 1. Read aloud and discuss *Here's the Idea.* Review the terms *character, setting,* and *plot.* Emphasize that the most important element among these three should be introduced in the introduction. Discuss briefly the meaning of *mood.*

2. Read the sample introduction in *Check It Out.* Ask the class to answer the questions who? what? and where?

3. Assign *Try Your Skill.* Note that the paragraph is written in first-person point of view and, therefore, can include details about thoughts and feelings. After discussing several of the students' paragraphs, assign *Now Write.*

Extending the Lesson Before the students revise their introductions for *Now Write,* have them exchange their papers with a partner. Each person should answer the following questions:

1. Who are the characters?
2. What is the setting?
3. Are any main events described?
4. What mood is created?

The writer of the paragraph can use the answers to pinpoint weaknessess; for example, the writer might have intended to create a sinister mood, yet he or she has given an entirely different impression to the reader.

Part 4 **Let's Have Action!** Developing a Narrative Composition
pp. 124-125

Objective To understand the importance of details to the development of plot and conflict

Presenting the Lesson 1. Read aloud and discuss *Here's the Idea.* Highlight the meanings of *plot* and *conflict.* Emphasize the importance of details in both true accounts and imaginary conflicts.

2. Read and discuss the sample paragraphs in *Check It Out.* Mention that the narrative could be either a true account or an imaginary story told from the first-person point of view.

3. Assign *Try Your Skill.* You might do the first sentence as a class exercise, asking such questions as these:

How might the rope be described?
How might the character feel?

Some students may need this kind of specific help for all of the sentences.

4. Assign *Now Write.*

Extending the Lesson Duplicate the paragraphs written by three students for *Try Your Skill.* Give copies to each member of the class. Have each student circle the specific details that were added.

Part 5 **Let's Talk** Using Dialogue in a Narrative pp. 126-127

Objective To gain skill in using dialogue to further plot development

Presenting the Lesson 1. Read aloud and discuss *Here's the Idea.* Note the mechanics of writing dialogue. Check comprehension by giving the class several examples of dialogue to write.

2. Read and discuss *Check It Out.* Review the mechanics. Point out the variety of explaining words used *(shouted, replied, insisted, answered, said).*

3. Assign *Try Your Skill.* Tell the students to write at least four exchanges of dialogue. After the class has completed this exercise, have the students read their dialogues to partners. Review mechanics.

4. Assign *Now Write.*

Extending the Lesson Choose two short comic strips from a local newspaper. Duplicate them and give copies to each member of the class. Have the students translate the dialogue for each comic strip into paragraph format.

Part 6 **Other Voices** Using Dialogue to Reveal Character pp. 128-129

Objective To gain skill in using dialogue to reveal character

Presenting the Lesson 1. Read aloud and discuss *Here's the Idea.*

Emphasize the importance of explaining words. Ask two volunteers to read the sample dialogue with the inflections called for by the explaining words. Note that the exclamation marks indicate enthusiasm.

2. Read and discuss the sample dialogue in *Check It Out*.

3. Assign *Try Your Skill*. Remind the class to use strong explaining words.

4. Assign *Now Write*.

Extending the Lesson Describe the following situations. Direct the students to write the dialogue requested for each.

1. Pepé and Carlos are both invited to their cousin's birthday party. Pepé loves parties and wants to go. Carlos hates parties, but knows he has to go to this one. Each calls his cousin to say he's coming. What might each person say?
2. Mary Joe and Jenny have received presents from their grandmother. Mary Jo opens her present and finds exactly what she wants—a blue sweater. What might she say? Jenny opens hers and finds a blue sweater instead of the roller skates that she wants. What might she say?
3. Sharon and Diane both have dogs that need washing. Sharon thinks it will be fun. Diane hates the job. What words might each person use when telling the dog it's time to take a bath?

Part 7 **Moving On** Using Transitions in a Narrative pp. 130-131

Objective To recognize and use transitions within and between the paragraphs of a narrative composition

Presenting the Lesson 1. Read aloud and discuss *Here's the Idea*. Emphasize the idea that transitions indicate time relationships.

2. Read and discuss the sample paragraph in *Check It Out*. After identifying the transitions in this paragraph, refer the class to the sample paragraphs in *Part 4, Check It Out*. Discuss the transitions within and between these paragraphs.

3. Assign *Try Your Skill.* Encourage the class to add details as well as transitions.

4. Assign *Now Write.*

Extending the Lesson Divide the class into groups of five or six students. Direct each group to name two characters, describe a setting, and outline a general situation. Then have one student in the group begin a story. The next student will continue the story and so on until everyone in the group has taken a turn. Each student must begin his or her portion of the narrative with a transition and must include at least one other transition as well.

Part 8 **The Finale** Completing a Narrative Composition
pp. 132-133

Objective To learn to complete a narrative composition with a strong conclusion and an interesting title

Presenting the Lesson 1. Read aloud and discuss *Here's the Idea.* Illustrate different types of conclusions by reading the final paragraphs of several short stories.

2. Read and discuss the sample paragraph in *Check It Out.* Point out the double meaning of the title.

3. Assign *Try Your Skill.* Some students may need to review the information about titles (presented in *Section 6, Part 6.*)

4. Assign *Now Write.* Remind the class to revise for mechanics as well as content. Tell the students to write three possible titles before choosing a final one. See number 1 in *Extending the Lesson* for an additional suggestion.

Extending the Lesson 1. Students who have difficulty choosing a title might submit their ideas to the entire class or to a small group made up of students who are having the same problem. Ask the class or group to choose the best title or to suggest other possibilities.

2. Encourage students to submit their compositions for inclusion in the second issue of the class magazine.

The Descriptive Composition

Pages 135-141

Objectives

1. To study and to practice the steps involved in planning a descriptive composition
2. To learn to write an effective introductory paragraph to a description
3. To understand the importance of sensory details in developing the body of a description
4. To gain skill in organizing a description in logical order
5. To learn to write a conclusion that summarizes the main idea of a composition and that includes feelings about the subject

Preparing the Students

Read aloud a short, factual account from a local newspaper. Ask the students to imagine that they were the reporter assigned to cover the story. Have them suggest things they might have seen, heard, smelled, touched, or tasted. Review the definition of *descriptive composition* (paragraphs that paint a picture with words).

Part 1 What Do You See? Planning a Descriptive Composition

pp. 136-137

Objective To study and to practice the steps involved in planning a descriptive composition

Presenting the Lesson 1. Read aloud and discuss *Here's the Idea.* On the chalkboard list the major steps presented:

Choose a topic.
List details.
Organize into spacial order.
Organize introduction, body, and conclusion.

Explain that these steps will be explained in greater detail in the following lessons.

2. Read and discuss the notes in *Check It Out*. Point out that the body paragraphs will focus on three major areas. Note the indications of spacial order in parentheses.

3. Assign *Try Your Skill*. Direct the class to put the body paragraphs in order also. Work in a small group with the students who have difficulty.

4. Assign *Now Write*. An exercise to use in assigning topics is described in *Extending the Lesson*.

Extending the Lesson Ask each student to write the name of one object or place familiar to the entire class on a slip of paper. These might be objects and places the children know first-hand, such as a neighborhood landmark or a local hangout, or objects and places they have read about or have seen on television. Collect the names. Have each student draw one slip of paper.

Part 2 **A Wider View** Using Sensory Details pp. 138-139

Objectives 1. To learn to write an effective introductory paragraph to a description

2. To understand the importance of sensory details in developing the body of a description

Presenting the Lesson 1. Read aloud and discuss *Here's the Idea*. Ask the students for examples of words and phrases that describe sensory details.

2. Read and discuss *Check It Out*. Remind the class that sensory details can be presented through adjectives and adverbs, strong verbs, and descriptive phrases.

3. Assign and discuss *Try Your Skill*.

4. Assign *Now Write*.

Extending the Lesson Ask students to imagine the same kitchen under these four circumstances:

1. In the morning when a family is busy making and eating breakfast
2. After a big party, before anyone has cleaned up
3. On a day when Dad bakes the bread for the week
4. Late at night when a person comes in for a midnight snack

Have each student write six details for each circumstance. The details should appeal to at least three senses.

Part 3 **How Do You Feel?** Organizing a Description
pp. 140-141

Objectives 1. To gain skill in organizing a description in logical order

2. To learn to write a conclusion that summarizes the main idea of a composition and that includes feelings about the subject

Presenting the Lesson 1. Read aloud and discuss *Here's the Idea.*

2. Read the first two sentences in *Check It Out.* Help students to recognize that the body paragraphs begin with the focal point (the bed) and move away from that point to the alcove in the far corner of the room. Complete the discussion of *Check It Out.*

3. Assign *Try Your Skill.* Encourage students to begin by grouping the objects into categories: what is outside, what is on the counter, what is behind the counter, and what is next to the counter.

4. Assign *Now Write.*

Extending the Lesson 1. Display five or six pictures. These can be scenes from *National Geographic, Arizona Highways,* or a similar magazine; reproductions of famous paintings; posters; or slides. They should represent a wide variety of subjects and visual compositions. Discuss with the class the most logical order for describing each picture.

2. Encourage students to submit their compositions for inclusion in the second issue of the class magazine.

WRITING SECTION 15

The Explanatory Composition

Telling *How* **Pages 143-149**

Objectives

1. To review the main characteristics of the explanatory *how* composition

2. To study the steps involved in planning an explanation
3. To gain skill in writing the introduction, body, and conclusion of a *how* composition
4. To understand the function of transitions within and between the paragraphs of a *how* composition

Preparing the Students

Prepare a classroom display of "how to" books and magazine articles. Leave room for additional materials. Point out the variety of subjects represented. Explain that in the next three lessons, the students will study the characteristics common to all explanations and will learn to write an explanation in composition format.

Part 1 **How Do You Do That?** Planning an Explanation

pp. 144-145

Objectives 1. To review the main characteristics of the explanatory *how* composition

2. To study the steps involved in planning an explanation

Presenting the Lesson 1. Read aloud and discuss *Here's the Idea.* Ask students for additional ideas of things to do or make. On the chalkboard list the following pre-writing steps:

Choose a topic.
List the steps and the materials and tools needed.
Write a title

2. Read and discuss the notes in *Check It Out.*
3. Assign *Try Your Skill.* Tell the class that at this point, they do not have to write the steps in order.
4. Assign *Now Write.*

Extending the Lesson Have each student find one explanation for how to do or make something. The sources can include books, magazine articles, game directions, cookbooks and recipes, and package directions on foods and toys. Add these to the classroom display. Encourage students who have difficulty finding a topic to use the display for ideas.

Part 2 **Step It Up** Using Step-by-Step Order pp. 146-147

Objective To gain skill in writing the introduction, body, and conclusion of a *how* composition

Presenting the Lesson 1. Read aloud and discuss *Here's the Idea.* Remind the class that compositions have three parts.

2. Read and discuss *Check It Out.* Refer the class to the notes in *Part 1, Check It Out.* Show how the notes were incorporated into the three paragraphs.

3. Assign and discuss *Try Your Skill.*

4. Assign *Now Write.* Some students may need help in arranging the steps in the process into three or four groups.

Extending the Lesson Duplicate a Rube Goldberg cartoon and give a copy to each member of the class. (Most city libraries contain a collection of Goldberg's cartoons or have reference books on cartoon art.) Direct students to list in order the steps pictured in the cartoon.

Part 3 **The Final Step** Using Transitions pp. 148-149

Objective To understand the function of transitions within and between the paragraphs of a *how* composition

Presenting the Lesson 1. Read aloud and discuss *Here's the Idea.* Emphasize that transitions clarify time order.

2. Read and discuss *Check It Out.* Ask a volunteer to read the entire composition.

3. Assign and discuss *Try Your Skill.* Point out that a variety of transitions can be used.

4. Assign *Now Write.*

Extending the Lesson 1. Direct students to exchange the compositions written for *Now Write* with a partner. Have each student read the composition and circle the transitions.

2. Choose three compositions. Duplicate them for the class. Ask each writer to demonstrate or pantomime the process explained while another student reads the written directions aloud. Discuss possible improvements.

3. Encourage students to contribute their compositions to the class magazine.

The Explanatory Composition

Telling *Why*

Pages 151-157

Objectives

1. To study the process of planning a composition that explains an opinion
2. To understand the need to support an opinion with reasons, presented in order of importance
3. To gain skill in using transitions to indicate order of importance
4. To learn to begin a *why* composition with an effective introductory paragraph and to end it with a summarizing conclusion

Preparing the Students

Review the difference between fact and opinion using these examples:

1. The school day ends at 3:00 P.M. (fact)
   School should end at 2:30 P.M. (opinion)
2. Frankenstein's monster is the subject of many movies. (fact)
   Frankenstein's monster is a pitiful character. (opinion)
3. Jogging is a popular exercise. (fact)
   Jogging is the best exercise. (opinion)

Ask the class for additional facts and opinions on the same subjects.

Part 1 For or Against? Stating an Opinion

pp. 152-153

Objective To study the process of planning a composition that explains an opinion

Presenting the Lesson 1. Read aloud and discuss *Here's the Idea.* Discuss answers to the questions posed in paragraph 2. On the chalkboard list the pre-writing steps described:

Choose a topic (write an opinion).
Take notes for the introduction.
Take notes for the body (list reasons or facts).
Take notes for the conclusion (summarize argument)

2. Read and discuss *Check It Out.* Note that three main reasons are given and that these reasons are developed with details.

3. Assign *Try Your Skill.* Remind the class to narrow the topics.

4. Assign *Now Write.* Suggest that students use the subject areas listed in *Try Your Skill* as a source for topic ideas.

Extending the Lesson Discuss the type of "person-on-the-street" interview in which passersby are asked for their opinions on a current topic. Divide the class into teams of three or four students. Direct each group to write an interview question. Set a time limit of two or three days during which the students will ask their questions of children from other classes, relatives, and neighbors and will record the answers.

Part 2 With Good Reasons Supporting an Opinion

pp. 154-155

Objective To understand the need to support an opinion with reasons, presented in order of importance

Presenting the Lesson 1. Read aloud and discuss *Here's the Idea.* Emphasize that reasons should be organized from the weakest to the strongest and that they should be presented in the body of the composition.

2. Read and discuss *Check It Out.* Refer the class to *Part 1, Check It Out.* Read the brief listing of reasons. Show how they were developed into the three paragraphs.

3. Assign and discuss *Try Your Skill.*

4. Assign *Now Write.*

Extending the Lesson 1. Choose a newspaper editorial in which the writer presents at least three reasons to support an opinion. (You may need to simplify the language somewhat.) Duplicate it and give a copy to each member of the class. Tell the students to do the following:

Write the opinion in your own words.
Underline each reason presented.

Number the reasons.
Star the most important reason.

2. Set aside a day or a half day for a field trip (or tell the class to imagine an ideal field trip). Have each student choose the place he or she would most like to visit and list three reasons in support of the choice. Discuss the suggestions and the strengths of the reasons. Vote on a destination.

Part 3 **Furthermore** Using Transitions pp. 156-157

Objectives 1. To gain skill in using transitions to indicate order of importance

2. To learn to begin a *why* composition with an effective introductory paragraph and to end it with a summarizing conclusion

Presenting the Lesson 1. Read aloud and discuss *Here's the Idea.* Highlight the two types of transitions and where each is most common.

2. Read and discuss *Check It Out.* Ask a volunteer to read the entire composition. Ask the class to identify the transitions in the body paragraphs.

3. Assign and discuss *Try Your Skill.*

4. Assign *Now Write.* Remind the students to check their body paragraphs for appropriate transitions.

Extending the Lesson 1. Duplicate two completed compositions and give a copy to each member of the class. Direct the students to do the following for the first composition:

Identify the title.
Draw two lines under the topic sentence for the entire composition.
Label the introduction, body, and conclusion.
Underline the main reasons.

Then direct the students to check the second composition for the following:

Indentation of each paragraph
Correct capitalization and punctuation
Correct spelling.
Complete sentences (no sentence fragments or run-on sentences).

2. Encourage students to contribute their compositions to the class magazine. With the help of a committee, compile the contributions, design the cover, write a table of contents, and duplicate the second issue. Distribute copies to the class.

WRITING SECTION 17

Writing Letters

Pages 159-171

Objectives

1. To review and to practice writing the five parts of a friendly letter
2. To learn to prepare and address an envelope
3. To study the form and content of invitations and thank-you notes
4. To gain skill in writing a correct business letter
5. To learn to write letters of request

Preparing the Students

Assign the following report topics:

1. Early postal systems in the United States
2. The Pony Express
3. Benjamin Franklin and the postal system
4. Processing a letter
5. Being a mail carrier
6. Stamp collecting

Introduce Section 17 by having students share their reports.

Part 1 **Write Soon** Writing a Friendly Letter pp. 160-162

Objective To review and to practice writing the five parts of a friendly letter

Presenting the Lesson 1. Read aloud and discuss *Here's the Idea.* Use the sample letter in *Check It Out* to illustrate each part.

2. Ask the class to identify the details in the sample letter.

3. Assign *Try Your Skill.*

4. Assign *Now Write.* Suggest that the students incorporate the sentences they wrote for *Try Your Skill* into their letters. After they have completed their letters, guide them in checking format, capitalization, and punctuation point by point.

Extending the Lesson Read aloud several examples of letters written by famous historical figures. Some classes might enjoy the "Letters to Horseface" series that was published in *Cricket* magazine or letters written by pioneers in the late eighteenth century. Discuss the interesting details included in each letter.

Part 2 Handle with Care Preparing Letters for the Mail pp. 163-164

Objective To learn to prepare and address an envelope

Presenting the Lesson 1. Read aloud and discuss *Here's the Idea.* Demonstrate the proper folding of a letter. Emphasize the importance of a correct and complete address.

2. Read and discuss *Check It Out.*

3. Assign *Try Your Skill.* After students have completed their envelopes, direct them to exchange papers and to check each other's addresses for accuracy of form and content.

Extending the Lesson 1. Ask a volunteer to visit the local post office to learn the following:

The differences among the classes of mail.

The regulations related to mailing packages.

2. Explain that some situations call for the inclusion of a "self-addressed stamped envelope." Discuss the meaning of that phrase. Have each student draw an envelope and address it to himself or herself.

Part 3 Special Occasions Writing Social Notes pp. 165-166

Objective To study the form and content of invitations and thank-you notes

Presenting the Lesson 1. Read aloud and discuss *Here's the Idea.* Explain the use and meaning of R.S.V.P. (at the bottom of an invitation, a request to please tell the person who is inviting you whether you are coming or not. In French, *Répondez, s'il vous plaît*)

2. Read and discuss *Check It Out.* Highlight the capitalization and punctuation.

3. Assign *Try Your Skill.* Check the completed letters for form and content. Have students revise and rewrite if necessary.

4. Assign *Now Write.* You may want to divide the class into three groups and assign one type of social note to each group. Discuss an example of each note.

Extending the Lesson Have each student describe an improbable situation on a slip of paper. Give the following as examples:

> You are a camel in a zoo. You have just been moved to a bigger cage and you are grateful. You want to write a thank-you note.
>
> Sir Frederick Fearless rescued you from an evil sorcerer. You rested at his castle for a week. You want to write a bread-and-butter note.
>
> You have won a million dollars in a contest. You want to write a note thanking the person who drew your name.

Collect the slips of paper. Have each student draw one and write the appropriate note.

Part 4 **Dear Sir or Madam:** Writing a Business Letter

pp. 167-169

Objective To gain skill in writing a correct business letter

Presenting the Lesson 1. Read aloud and discuss *Here's the Idea.* Show the class several examples of business letters. Ask them to identify the form followed in each. You may need to introduce the term *letterhead* and to explain that a letterhead takes the place of a heading.

2. Read and discuss *Check It Out.* Highlight the capitalization and punctuation of the sample letter.

3. Assign *Try Your Skill.* Ask several volunteers to read their completed letters to the class.

4. Assign *Now Write.* Have each student draw an envelope and address it to go along with the letter.

Extending the Lesson With the class, prepare a checklist that details the specifics of capitalization and punctuation in a business letter. Save the checklist for use in the following lesson.

Part 5 **Information, Please** Writing a Letter of Request

pp. 170-171

Objective To learn to write letters of request

Presenting the Lesson 1. Read aloud and discuss *Here's the Idea.* Emphasize the importance of brevity, accuracy, and politeness.

2. Read and discuss *Check It Out.* Review the six parts of a business letter.

3. Assign and discuss *Try Your Skill.* Select one letter for actual mailing.

4. Assign *Now Write.* Have the students write a first draft, revise it using the checklist prepared for the previous lesson, and make a final copy.

Extending the Lesson Divide the class into seven groups. Assign each one a major geographical area of the United States: New England, Middle Atlantic States, South, Midwest, West, Southwest, and Pacific Northwest. Direct each group to use a map or an encyclopedia to find the name of a major national park in that area and to write a letter requesting information from that park.

WRITING SECTION 18

Using a Dictionary

Pages 173-181

Objectives

1. To review the basic characteristics of a dictionary
2. To understand that guide words are aids to locating definitions

3. To practice interpreting the information contained in dictionary entries
4. To gain skill in using context to determine the applicable definition of a word

Preparing the Students

Assess the students' knowledge of dictionaries by asking the following:

1. How are the words arranged?
2. What information is given about each word?
3. What are guide words? How are they used?
4. What do the following abbreviations mean: *v*, *n.*, *adv.*, *adj.*, *s.*, *pl.*?
5. How many syllables make up the following word?

   en thu si as´ tic

   Which syllable is accented?

Part 1 **Word for Word** Using a Dictionary pp. 174-175

Objective To review the basic characteristics of a dictionary

Presenting the Lesson 1. Read aloud and discuss *Here's the Idea.* Compare an abridged dictionary with an unabridged dictionary. Find three words in the unabridged that are not in the abridged. Refer students to their classroom dictionaries. Discuss the abbreviations and symbols listed in the front.

2. Read and discuss *Check It Out.* Choose two of the words and have the students look them up in their classroom dictionaries. Note differences between the abbreviations and symbols used and variations in the wording of the meanings.

3. Assign and discuss *Try Your Skill.*

4. Assign *Now Write.*

Extending the Lesson Give the class these three sentences:

1. A teacher will *chide* a tardy pupil.
2. The ruler was *autocratic.*
3. The climbers reached the *pinnacle.*

For each underlined word, have the students do the following:

Find it in the dictionary.
Write the word that appears before it and the one that appears after it.
Rewrite the sentence, substituting a synonym for the word.

Part 2 **Follow the Signs** Using Guide Words pp. 176-177

Objective To understand that guide words are aids to locating definitions

Presenting the Lesson 1. Read aloud and discuss *Here's the Idea.* Have the class find *music* in their own dictionaries and identify the guide words at the top of the page.

2. Discuss the answers to the questions in *Check It Out.*

3. Assign *Try Your Skill.* Work in a small group with the students who have difficulty with this exercise.

4. Assign *Now Write.*

Extending the Lesson To help students gain speed in using guide words, play the following game:

1. To prepare:

Divide the chalkboard into five columns.
Choose five dictionary pages.
At the top of each column, write the guide words from one of the dictionary pages.
On index cards write words from the five pages. Prepare more cards than there are students.
Divide the class into teams of five or six students. The teams must have equal numbers of students.
Place a pile of six or more cards, face down, in front of each team.

2. To play:

The first student in each team draws a card from the team's pile.
The student writes the word on the chalkboard in the correct column.
The student returns to his seat.
The next student does the same thing.
The team that finishes first wins the game.

Part 3 **Read All About It** Reading a Dictionary Entry pp. 178-179

Objective To practice interpreting the information contained in dictionary entries

Presenting the Lesson 1. Read aloud and discuss *Here's the Idea.* As each part of a dictionary entry is described, refer the students to their classroom dictionaries. Note any differences in content, abbreviations, or symbols. Students should be using dictionaries that include etymologies.

2. Read and answer the questions about the dictionary entry in *Check It Out.*

3. Assign and discuss *Try Your Skill.* Work in a small group with students who have difficulty with this exercise.

4. Assign *Now Write.*

Extending the Lesson Have each student page through a dictionary to find an unfamiliar word. Tell the class to copy the first two meanings in the entry. Then have them make up an entry for the same word. The new entry should imitate the style of the correct one, but contain incorrect information. Direct the students to exchange papers with a partner and to guess which of each other's entries is correct.

Part 4 **A Good Fit** Finding the Meaning of a Word pp. 180-181

Objective To gain skill in using context to determine the applicable definition of a word

Presenting the Lesson 1. Read aloud and discuss *Here's the Idea.* Have the class find the four definitions for *eye* in their classroom dictionaries.

2. Answer the question in *Check It Out.* Ask volunteers to use the word *space* in other contexts.

3. Assign and discuss *Try Your Skill.*

4. Assign *Now Write.*

Extending the Lesson Direct the students to find each of the following words in the dictionary and to copy two meanings.

game	cap
count	clutch
pelt	pass
drop	swing
pick	grate

Have them write a sentence for each meaning.

WRITING SECTION 19

Using the Library

Pages 183-191

Objectives

1. To review the library system for arranging and shelving fiction and nonfiction books
2. To gain skill in using the library's card catalog
3. To increase knowledge about the organization and content of encyclopedias

Preparing the Students

Discuss briefly the occasions on which students have used the school or public library. Mention examples of the different places where information is stored in a library. They include books, encyclopedias, pamphlets, records, magazines, newspapers, photographs, and microfilm. Explain that the following lessons focus on the materials the students use most often—books and encyclopedias.

Part 1 A Good Place To Visit Using the Library
pp. 184-186

Objective To review the library system for arranging and shelving fiction and nonfiction books

Presenting the Lesson 1. Read aloud and discuss *Here's the Idea.* Ask the class to explain the difference between fiction and nonfiction books. Show several examples of each. Note the call numbers on the spines of the nonfiction books.

2. If a library that the students use regularly classifies books by the Library of Congress System, you will need to provide the class with those classification categories. Emphasize that the basic process of grouping books by subject, assigning numbers, then shelving the books by number is the same as in the Dewey Decimal System.

3. Discuss *Check It Out.* Ask the class to name the category of each nonfiction book and the author's last name for each fiction book.

4. Assign and discuss *Try Your Skill.* For further practice in arranging books, assign the exercise described in *Extending the Lesson.*

5. Assign *Now Write.* Have the students include the authors of the fiction books and the authors and call numbers of the nonfiction books.

Extending the Lesson Choose twelve or fourteen book titles, five fiction and the rest nonfiction, from the students' *Now Write* selections. Make up a worksheet on which the titles, authors, and, for the nonfiction books, the call numbers appear as they would on the spines of the books. Direct the students to cut apart the worksheet, to separate the fiction and nonfiction books, to arrange each group of books as they would be arranged on the shelves, and to paste or tape the books in order on two separate sheets of paper.

Part 2 **Card Tricks** Using the Card Catalog pp. 187-189

Objective To gain skill in using the library's card catalog

Presenting the Lesson 1. Read aloud and discuss *Here's the Idea.* Emphasize that the same information is included on each type of card. Use the three samples to illustrate. Emphasize the differences in the arrangement of information. Explain that the library system does not capitalize important words in a title.

2. Discuss the answers to the questions in *Check It Out.*

3. Assign *Try Your Skill.* Display examples of each type of card on a bulletin board. You may want to ditto enough cards for the class.

4. Assign *Now Write.*

Extending the Lesson Direct each student to choose two books, one fiction and one nonfiction, from the worksheet prepared for *Part 1, Extending the Lesson.* Have students find in the card catalog two cards for each book and copy the information from each card.

Part 3 **It's All There** Using an Encyclopedia pp. 190-191

Objective To increase knowledge about the organization and content of encyclopedias

Presenting the Lesson 1. Read aloud and discuss *Here's the Idea.*

2. Discuss the answers to the questions in *Check It Out.* If your classroom has a set of encyclopedias, ask the class to name the volume where each item of information can be found. See the entry *Mark Twain* for an example of a cross-reference.

3. Assign and discuss *Try Your Skill.*

4. Assign *Now Write.*

Extending the Lesson Tell each student to list the general encyclopedias in the school or public library. (The public library probably offers a wider selection.) Have students find the same topic in each encyclopedia. After looking at all the encyclopedias, tell them to circle on their lists the ones whose reading levels are beyond their comprehension, to underline any that seem too easy, and to star the one that seems best for them.

Learning About Sentences

Pages 207-300

Objectives

1. To distinguish between fragments and complete sentences
2. To identify the four kinds of sentences:
   declarative imperative
   interrogative exclamatory
3. To use the correct end punctuation for each kind of sentence
4. To identify and form the two basic sentence parts: subject and predicate
5. To understand the function of the verb (simple predicate) and to identify verbs in sentences
6. To differentiate between main verbs and helping verbs
7. To identify and use verbs with separated parts
8. To understand the term *simple subject* and to identify simple subjects in sentences with regular word order
9. To identify subjects in unusual positions
10. To identify subjects in interrogative and exclamatory sentences
11. To be aware of the understood subject of imperative sentences
12. To identify and form compound subjects
13. To identify and form compound predicates
14. To recognize the usual word order of sentences

Preparing the Students

Follow these directions to prepare several large puzzles for use in a class exercise.

1. Cut out a large picture from a newspaper or magazine.
2. Paste the picture on heavy paper or cardboard.
3. Cut the picture lengthwise into two pieces, making an interlocking puzzle-edge design.

4. Write a sentence on the back of the picture, one sentence part per piece, based on the content of the picture.

Front

Back

Distribute puzzle pieces to members of the class. Have them find the matching pieces and form the complete picture and sentence. Discuss how the picture had to be arranged in a certain way to make it complete. Relate the completed picture to the composition of the sentence on the back. Remind students that a sentence is a group of words that expresses a complete thought.

Explain that this chapter will help them to understand and write good sentences. Read aloud and discuss the introduction on page 207.

Part 1 Complete Sentences pp. 208-209

Objective To distinguish between fragments and complete sentences

Presenting the Lesson 1. Read the text on pages 208 to 209. Discuss the concept of sentence fragments and what is needed to make complete sentences.

2. Ask students to match the following sentence parts to form complete sentences. Do not discourage humorous combinations. They will help to reinforce the need for careful sentence composition in serious writing.

that white rabbit
the TV repairman
ran past the matador
munched on a carrot
bloomed in the garden
a charging bull
some yellow daisies
fixed our broken television

3. Devise a quick, oral drill using phrases suggested by things or people in the classroom—*"Bill's notebook," "sharpened a pencil."* Have students add words to make complete sentences.

4. Assign and discuss Exercises A and B on page 209.

Part 2 Four Kinds of Sentences pp. 210-212

Objectives 1. To identify the four kinds of sentences:

declarative imperative
interrogative exclamatory

2. To use the correct end punctuation for each kind of sentence

Presenting the Lesson 1. Read and discuss page 210. Point out that students are probably familiar with other names for the four kinds of sentences.

declarative = statement
interrogative = question
imperative = command or request
exclamatory = exclamation

2. Do Exercise A on pages 210 and 211 aloud with the class. Assign and discuss Exercise B.

3. Read and discuss Punctuating Sentences on page 211. Stress the importance of careful end punctuation for sentences.

4. Assign and discuss Exercises A and B on pages 211 and 212.

Extending the Lesson Demonstrate the differences in the four kinds of sentences by reading the following sentences aloud with expression.

Declarative: I want an apple.
Interrogative: Do you want an apple?
Imperative: Please give me an apple.
Exclamatory: What a delicious apple this is!

Have students read the sentences in the Exercises on pages 211 and 212 aloud and with expression.

Part 3 Every Sentence Has Two Parts pp. 212-215

Objective To identify and form the two basic sentence parts: subject and predicate.

Presenting the Lesson 1. Read and discuss pages 212 and 213.

2. Stress that the usual sentence pattern is subject followed by predicate. Examples:

Subject	Predicate
The large dog	scared my baby sister.
Thunderstorms	occur often in spring.
Two different answers	confused us.

3. Assign and discuss Exercises A and B on page 214. It is suggested that Exercises C and D on pages 214 and 215 be done orally.

Optional Practice Use Exercises C and D on pages 214 and 215 for a small group oral activity. Each member of the group is to complete each sentence with an appropriate predicate or subject, different from those already stated.

Extending the Lesson Have students create a set of subject and predicate flash cards. They can be used for individual practice or for a classroom activity.

Part 4 The Verb

pp. 215-230

Objectives 1. To understand the function of the verb (simple predicate) and to identify verbs in sentences.

2. To differentiate between main verbs and helping verbs
3. To identify and use verbs with separated parts

Presenting the Lesson 1. This Part is to be covered in at least three separate lessons: The Verb and Finding the Verb (steps 2 to 4); Main Verbs and Helping Verbs (steps 5 to 7); and Separated Parts of the Verb (Steps 8 to 10).

2. Read and discuss pages 215 and 216. Stress the fact that *verb* and *simple predicate* are both names for the same thing. Point out that the verb is only a part of the complete predicate in most sentences.

3. If a student raises the question, explain that the verb may be more than one word long. However, in this lesson, all verbs are one word long. (Verbs consisting of more than one word will be presented in the next lesson of this Part.)

4. Assign and discuss Exercises A and B on page 216.

5. Read and discuss pages 217 and 218.

6. Students should become familiar with all the listed helping verbs. Special attention should be paid to those verbs that can be used either as main verbs or as helping verbs.

Some students may challenge the rule that certain verbs can be used only as helping verbs. They may point out that the following is an acceptable sentence: *I can.* However, that sentence is not complete in itself. Its meaning depends on its context.

Examples: Can you ski?
I can (ski).
Can you knit?
I can (knit).
Can you type?
I can (type).

When *can* is used alone, it is still a helping verb. Its main verb is known from the sentences preceding it, and simply understood.

7. Assign Exercises A and B on pages 218 and 219.

8. Read and discuss page 219. Pay particular attention to the verb contractions. Stress that the *n't* is not considered part of the verb.

9. Students will often incorrectly identify adverbs as helping verbs, especially those in positions between helping verbs and main verbs. Suggest that students review the lists of helping verbs on page 218. Most helping verbs are included there.

10. You may feel that students who experience difficulty with Main Verbs and Helping Verbs should not be assigned Separated Parts of the Verb. If so, have these students use the time for additional practice on identifying helping verbs and main verbs not separated by adverbs.

11. Assign and discuss Exercises A and B on page 220.

Optional Practice Students who are having difficulty should identify the complete predicate for each sentence in the Exercises on pages 218, 219, and 220 before looking for the helping verbs and main verbs.

Extending the Lesson 1. How many different sentences can be created from this base sentence by adding helping verbs, changing the verb form where necessary?

The dog barked.

2. This activity is suggested only for those students who understand the role of the verb in the sentence.

Each sentence pair below uses a particular word two ways. In one of the sentences, the underlined word is a verb. In the other it is not. Have the student choose the sentence in each pair whose underlined word is a verb.

1. a. The charge for the meal was low.
   b. The cavalry charged up the hill.
2. a. Run home and get your baseball mitt.
   b. He scored a run in the first inning of the game.
3. a. That light is too bright.
   b. Light a match.
4. a. Please set the alarm clock.
   b. I bought a paint set.
5. a. They drive to Florida every year.
   b. The drive home seemed long.

Part 5 The Simple Subject pp. 221-222

Objective To understand the term *simple subject* and to identify simple subjects in sentences with regular word order

Presenting the Lesson 1. Read and discuss page 221.

2. Ask students to suggest other sentences. Have the class identify the simple subjects.

3. Assign and discuss Exercises A and B on pages 221 and 222.

Extending the Lesson Use this activity only with those students who understand the difference between the subject and the verb.

Have students write two sentences for each of the following words, first using the word as a simple subject and then using the word as a verb:

box plant light play trap

Part 6 The Subject in Unusual Positions pp. 222-224

Objective To identify subjects in unusual positions

Presenting the Lesson 1. Do not assign this section to students who are still experiencing difficulty identifying the subject in usual positions. Provide additional practice with subject identification in regular sentence patterns.

2. Read and discuss pages 222 and 223.

3. In working with subjects in unusual positions, emphasize that students first locate the verb in the sentence.

4. Assign and discuss Exercises A and B on pages 223 and 224. It may help to invert some of the sentences before analyzing them. Be sure that students understand Part 6 before proceeding with Part 7.

Part 7 Subjects and Verbs in Interrogative and Exclamatory Sentences pp. 224-225

Objective To identify subjects in interrogative and exclamatory sentences

Presenting the Lesson 1. Review interrogative and exclamatory sentences as explained in Part 2 on pages 210 and 211.

2. Read and discuss page 224. Point out that a given sentence may be rewritten into several patterns, to suit the style of the writer.

3. It is recommended that you do Exercise A on page 225 with the class. Assign Exercise B only to the more advanced students.

Part 8 When the Subject Is Not Given pp. 226-227

Objective To be aware of the understood subject of imperative sentences

Presenting the Lesson 1. Before the lesson, write the following sentence on the board:

Please open your book to page 226.

Ask students to identify the verb in the sentence (*open*). Ask them *who* or *what* is supposed to do the opening. They should easily see that they themselves are being indicated. The subject, the person being asked to do something, is always understood to be the word *you*.

2. Read and discuss page 226.

3. It is suggested that the class do Exercise A on page 226 together. Have students identify each sentence by kind: declarative, interrogative, imperative, or exclamatory. Assign and discuss Exercise B on pages 226 and 227.

Part 9 Compound Subjects
pp. 227-229

Objective To identify and form compound subjects

Presenting the Lesson 1. Read and discuss pages 227 and 228. Stress that *compound* means "more than one."

2. Point out that the conjunctions *and* and *or* can both be used to form compound subjects, but that they have different meanings.

3. Assign Exercises A and B on pages 228 and 229. Discuss the various possible answers. Note that other words may come between the words of the compound subject.

Extending the Lesson Rewrite each of the following sentence pairs as a single sentence with a compound subject.

1. Tom earned an A in math.
   Amy earned an A in math.
2. My aunt visited the Grand Canyon.
   My cousin visited the Grand Canyon.
3. The rabbit ate the lettuce.
   The gerbil ate the lettuce.
4. Many rainstorms occur in April.
   Many windstorms occur in April.
5. Sandwiches are served for lunch.
   Salads are served for lunch.

Part 10 Compound Predicates
pp. 229-230

Objective To identify and form compound predicates

Presenting the Lesson 1. Read and discuss page 229.

2. Discuss the different meanings of the conjunctions *and, but,* and *or.*

3. It is suggested that you do at least part of Exercise A on page 230 aloud with the class. Assign and discuss the rest of Exercise A, and Exercise B.

Extending the Lesson Rewrite each of the following pairs of sentences as a single sentence with a compound predicate.

1. The poodle ran around the yard.
   The poodle jumped over the fence.
2. Marla cut out the dress pattern.
   Marla sewed the dress.

3. My pen fell to the floor.
   My pen spilled all its ink.
4. Eric called the restaurant.
   Eric ordered a pizza.
5. The science club held a contest.
   The science club awarded a prize.

Sentence Patterns Word Order and Meaning p. 231

Objective To recognize the usual word order of sentences

Presenting the Lesson 1. Ask the class to listen carefully and follow the instructions below. Read them no more than twice, and wait for the students to figure them out.

1. Books your open.
2. Find 231 page.

Explain that their difficulty in understanding was caused by the unusual word order in the directions.

2. Read and discuss page 231.
3. Assign and discuss the Exercise on page 231.

Optional Practice Encourage students to make their own picture puzzles like the ones at the beginning of the chapter. Have students work with them to reinforce their understanding of complete sentences.

Review p. 232

You may use the review on page 232 either as a checkup or for additional practice.

Using Sentences Correctly Pages 233-239

Objectives

1. To avoid or correct sentence fragments
2. To avoid or correct run-on sentences

Preparing the Students

Remind students that in Section 1 they learned what makes a complete sentence and how to punctuate it. Review the definition of a sentence and its two major parts. Explain that this chapter will contain more about how to write correct sentences and how to avoid some common mistakes.

Read the introduction on pages 233 and 234. Discuss the meaning of *fragment* and *run-on* sentence.

Part 1 Avoiding Sentence Fragments pp. 234-236

Objective To avoid or correct sentence fragments

Presenting the Lesson 1. Read and discuss pages 234 and 235. Stress that a fragment may be changed to a good sentence by adding words to complete the thought.

2. Assign and discuss Exercises A and B on page 235. It is suggested that you do Exercise C on page 236 with the class.

Optional Practice Have students correct all fragments in Exercises A and B by adding whatever words are needed. For each item, ask for several sentence completions, from different students. Help the class see that each student got a different idea about the fragment because the fragment itself did not give a complete idea.

Part 2 Avoiding Run-on Sentences pp. 236-238

Objective To avoid or correct run-on sentences

Presenting the Lesson 1. Read and discuss pages 236 and 237. Explain that there is more than one way to correct a run-on. Review end punctuation if necessary. Stress that when a run-on sentence is broken into parts, each part must tell a complete idea.

2. It is suggested that you do Exercise A on page 237 with the class. Make sure the students can identify where the first idea in a run-on sentence ends. Assign and discuss Exercises B and C on pages 237 and 238.

Optional Practice Have students correct all run-on sentences in Exercises A and B.

Review

p. 239

You may use the review on page 239 either as a checkup or for additional practice.

HANDBOOK SECTION 3

Using Nouns

Pages 240-251

Objectives

1. To understand the concept of the noun
2. To identify nouns in sentences
3. To differentiate between common and proper nouns
4. To differentiate between singular and plural nouns
5. To apply general rules for forming plural nouns
6. To use the dictionary to find irregular plural forms of specific words
7. To use the appropriate methods of forming possessive forms of nouns
8. To recognize the basic word order in the NV sentence pattern

Preparing the Students

Ask the students if any of them have very young sisters or brothers. Have them list some of the first words learned by the infants. Point out that the majority of those first words are names of people and things: *Mama, Dada, blanket.* Explain that in this chapter they will learn more about this group of words.

Part 1 Using Nouns

pp. 240-242

Objectives 1. To understand the concept of the noun
2. To identify nouns in sentences

Presenting the Lesson 1. Read pages 240 and 241. Discuss the three types of nouns. Make sure that students understand that nouns are not limited to physical objects. Ask students to supply additional examples of all types of nouns.

2. In addition to the definition of a noun given in this Chapter, there are other ways to identify a noun. The following chart, Ways To Identify Nouns, is based on what linguists have discovered about the structure of a word and the order of the words in a sentence. It is suggested that the information in the chart be used to point out additional ways in which nouns function.

Ways To Identify Nouns

1. Look for words that have a singular, plural, or possessive form.

Singular	Plural	Possessive
girl	girls	girl's

2. Look for words that follow *a, an,* or *the.*

   The *table* was made of pine.

3. Look for words that fit the blanks in one of these test sentences:

   ________ are very important.
   That is a ________.
   See the ________.
   Put it near the ________.

3. Assign and discuss Exercises A, B, and C on pages 241 and 242.

Optional Practice Have students try their answers to Exercises A and B in the test sentences in Presenting the Lesson. Do students discover any errors?

Extending the Lesson Ask students to list as many nouns as they can that refer to themselves, or to where they live.

Examples:	boy	apartment
	son	building
	player	Chicago
	student	Illinois
	friend	United States

Part 2 Common Nouns and Proper Nouns pp. 242-244

Objective To differentiate between common nouns and proper nouns

Presenting the Lesson 1. Read and discuss pages 242 and 243.

2. Ask students to think of additional examples of proper nouns in each of the three categories. If they experience difficulty, suggest that they think of people they read about or see on TV, and places they have visited or would like to visit. Be flexible in assigning categories; a term may fit in more than one.

3. It is recommended that Exercise A on page 243 be done as a class activity. Assign and discuss the remaining exercises.

Extending the Lesson Ask students to bring short newspaper articles to class. Have them circle all proper nouns and underline all common nouns. If possible, duplicate one article for class discussion. Do students discover any capitalization errors in the newspaper?

Part 3 Singular and Plural Nouns pp. 244-247

Objectives 1. To differentiate between singular and plural nouns

2. To apply general rules for forming plural nouns

3. To use the dictionary to find plural forms of specific words

Presenting the Lesson 1. Read and discuss page 244. Make sure the students recognize the difference between singular and plural nouns, and between a singular noun and its plural form. Ask for examples of each class.

2. Read the rules on page 245. Ask for additional examples to support each rule.

3. Read and discuss Using a Dictionary To Find Plurals, on pages 245 and 246. If students have access to individual dictionaries, ask for suggestions of nouns whose plurals are hard to predict. Have the students look up each word and find the plural form. (Possible nouns: ox, goose, loaf, piano, fish)

4. Assign and discuss Exercises A and B on pages 246 and 247.

Optional Practice Students may complete the following exercise for practice. Choose the correct plural form.

1. Three (mouse/mice) ate the cheese.
2. Those (leaves/leafs) blew into the gutter.
3. Give the (toyes/toys) to the small child.
4. The weather warning covers four (counties/countys).
5. The bells of all the (churchs/churches) rang at noon.

Extending the Lesson Write the following nouns on the board. Students should identify the nouns that are singular, and be able to give the plural form of each. Then they should identify the plural nouns, and give the singular form for each.

pens	leaf
flower	banjo
half	cherry
faces	coaches
buggies	parades

Part 4 How Nouns Show Possession pp. 247-249

Objective To use the appropriate methods of forming possessive forms of nouns

Presenting the Lesson 1. Read and discuss pages 247 and 249.

2. Emphasize the importance of first deciding if a word is singular or plural before checking its possessive spelling.

3. Assign and discuss Exercise A on pages 248 and 249. It is suggested that the class do Exercise B together. Assign and discuss Exercise C.

Optional Practice Have students rewrite the following words in their possessive forms. Cursive writing should be used.

Julie	window	player	lady	child
books	king	cities	oxen	temple

Extending the Lesson 1. An important proofreading skill is knowing when a sentence requires a possessive form and when it does not. Ask the students to select the correct word for each sentence.

1. Several (boys/boy's) played baseball in the park.
2. My (sisters/sister's) class went on a field trip.
3. The volume (control's/controls) are broken.
4. Seven (students/student's) won prizes in the contest.
5. Our (cat/cat's) food dishes were empty.

2. Ask students to bring in newspaper clippings showing possessive forms. Advertisements are especially good—for example, *a sale of boys' clothes.* Circle all possessives and display on bulletin board or with overhead projector.

Sentence Patterns The NV Pattern p. 250

Objective To recognize the basic word order in the N V sentence pattern

Presenting the Lesson 1. Read and discuss page 250. As the chart indicates, the noun-part of each sentence includes not only the noun identified as the subject, but also all the modifiers of that noun. The verb-part includes the verb and its modifiers, if any (as in *Carl ate quickly*). The students should be able to identify the point at which a sentence can be divided into these two parts.

2. Assign and discuss Exercises A and C. It is suggested that the class do Exercise B together.

Extending the Lesson The following lengthy sentences are basic N V pattern sentences. Ask students to identify the break between the noun-part and the verb-part.

1. My very funny Aunt Sarah jokes with us constantly.
2. Several gray squirrels ran across the yard and up the tree.
3. Those two players with green and white uniforms scored during the first half of the game.

Review

p. 251

You may use the review on page 251 either as a checkup or for additional practice.

HANDBOOK SECTION 4

Using Verbs

Pages 252-270

Objectives

1. To identify verbs as either action words or state-of-being words
2. To recognize common helping verbs and their main verbs
3. To identify direct objects and to understand their relationship to verbs
4. To understand the concept of linking verbs
5. To identify both linking verbs and words they link to the subject in sentences
6. To distinguish between direct objects and predicate words
7. To understand the concepts of the three simple tenses of verbs: present, past, and future
8. To recognize and use the simple tenses
9. To recognize the basic word order in the N V N, N LV N, and N LV Adj sentence patterns

Preparing the Students

Part 4 of Section 1 has already introduced the verb. If much time has passed since the study of Section 1, you may wish to review subjects and predicates now. Ask students to identify the complete subject and predicate for each of these sentences.

1. The first five customers received prizes.
2. The thunder and lightning frightened our dog.

Read and discuss page 252.

Part 1 Kinds of Verbs

pp. 253-254

Objective To identify verbs as either action verbs or state-of-being verbs

Presenting the Lesson 1. Read and discuss page 253. Make a clear distinction between action verbs and state-of-being verbs. Action verbs are more easily understood and recognized. Additional practice with state-of-being verbs may be needed.

2. In addition to the general definition of a verb given in the text, there are other ways to identify a verb. These ways, listed in the following chart, are based on what linguists have discovered about the structure of a word and the order of words in a sentence. It is suggested that the information in the chart be used to point out additional ways in which verbs function.

Ways to Identify Verbs

1. Look for words that change their forms to show past time.

Present	**Past**
walk	walked
eat	ate

2. Look for words that follow helping verbs (forms of *be, do, have,* and helping verbs such as *can, could, shall, will, may, might,* and *must).*
3. Look for words with the following endings or suffices:

   -ify (clarify) *-ize (realize)*
4. Look for words that fit the blank in this test sentence:

   Please __________.

3. Ask students to identify the state-of-being verb in each of these sentences:

1. That award is a high honor.
2. We are happy with our new car.
3. The position was very important.
4. Lee's mother is a doctor.
5. My family is proud.

4. Point out the special use of these state-of-being verbs:

be—used only when preceded by a helping verb: *can, could, shall, should, would, may, might, must, will*

being—used only when preceded by a *be* word as a helping verb: *is, am, are, was, were*

been—used only when preceded by a *have* word: *have, has, had*

5. It is suggested that Exercises A and B on pages 253 and 254 be done as a class activity. Assign and discuss Exercise C.

Optional Practice Ask students to write sentences using each of the following words as a verb (use no helping verbs):

sing   skates   write   thought   take

Extending the Lesson Collect a set of interesting action pictures from newspapers and magazines. Number the pictures. Pass them around the room and ask students to think of one verb suggested by each picture. When all students have finished their lists, write all the suggestions for each picture on the board. Can each be used in a sentence as a verb? Discuss them.

Part 2 Main Verbs and Helping Verbs pp. 255-257

Objective To recognize common helping verbs and their main verbs

Presenting the Lesson 1. Read and discuss pages 255 and 256. Give special attention to the difference between the use of verbs as helping verbs and as main verbs. In the examples showing *is* and *has* as helping verbs, point out the main verb as well. Use the following sentence for practice. Have the students tell whether the italicized word is a helping verb or a main verb.

1. That tree *is* swaying in the breeze.
2. The winner *was* Mary Robertson.
3. Everyone *did* the lesson perfectly.
4. My new pen *is* already dry.
5. I *have* given that idea some serious thought.

2. It is suggested that Exercise A on pages 256 and 257 be done as a class activity. Assign and discuss Exercise B.

Extending the Lesson Have students use each of the *be, have,* and *do* words listed on page 255 in two sentences. Use the word first as a helping verb and then as a main verb. Discuss the sentences.

Part 3 Verbs and Direct Objects

pp. 257-260

Objective To identify direct objects and to understand their relationship to verbs

Presenting the Lesson 1. Read aloud and discuss pages 257 and 258. Most students will recognize that the word functioning as a direct object is usually a noun. Avoid discussion of pronouns as direct objects until after the study of Section 7.

2. Emphasize that the direct object receives the action of a verb. A verb that has a direct object must be an action verb, not a state-of-being verb.

3. It is suggested that you work with the class the first Exercise, A, under both sets of Exercises (Add direct objects, pages 258 and 259, and Find direct objects, page 259). Assign and discuss both Exercises B, on pages 259 and 260.

Extending the Lesson Use each of the following words in two sentences. In the first sentence, use it as the subject. In the second sentence, use it as the direct object.

spaceship   sandwich   book   basketball   song

Part 4 Linking Verbs

pp. 260-264

Objectives 1. To understand the concept of linking verbs

2. To identify linking verbs and the words they link to the subjects in sentences

3. To distinguish between direct objects and predicate words

Presenting the Lesson 1. Read and discuss pages 260 and 261.

2. Emphasize that linking verbs are not action verbs. They simply tell that something is, or exists. They are always followed by an adjective or a noun. At this time, do not develop the definition of adjectives beyond the fact that they are words that may describe the subject. Adjectives will be presented in detail in Section 8. In this Part, the emphasis should be on the linking verb,

rather than the word linked to the subject. Avoid the discussion of pronouns after linking verbs until after the study of Section 7. Carefully discuss the examples on page 261.

It may be helpful to mention that since a predicate adjective describes the subject, it is usually possible to use that same adjective before the subject. For example, *These cookies taste delicious* tells about *delicious cookies*.

3. Exercise A on page 261 may be done orally if students appear to be experiencing difficulty. Assign and discuss Exercise B on page 262.

4. Read and discuss pages 262 and 263. Emphasize the importance of finding the verb before attempting to identify other parts of the sentence.

5. It is suggested that you do Exercise A on page 263 together. Assign Exercise B on pages 263 and 264.

Extending the Lesson 1. Ask students to use each of the following verbs in two sentences. In the first sentence, use it as an action verb. In the second sentence, use it as a linking verb.

taste	feel	look
grow	appear	sound

2. Have students use each of the following words as the direct object in a sentence.

robot job kangaroo doctor beard

3. Have students use each of the following words as either a predicate noun or a predicate adjective in a sentence.

canoe math loud brother clever

Part 5 **Verb Tenses** pp. 264-265

Objectives 1. To understand the concepts of the three simple tenses of verbs: present, past, and future

2. To recognize and use the simple tenses

Presenting the Lesson 1. Read and discuss page 264. Provide additional examples for each of the simple tenses. Have students create sentences for each.

2. Ask students to add examples to each of the methods listed at the bottom of page 264.

3. Read aloud and discuss page 265. Be sure the students realize that the present tense has two forms: one used with singular subjects, that ends in *-s* or *-es*, and one used with plural subjects, that does not end in *-s* or *-es*. The future tense uses the second form.

4. Demonstrate the natural formation of regular verb past tense with a nonsense word example.

> The teams *gronch* onto the field.
> Yesterday the teams________. *(gronched?)*

Most students will automatically follow the regular *-ed* pattern. Point out that small children learning the language often naturally follow the regular verb form when the irregular verb form really applies (as in *goed, eated, drinked,* or *runned.*)

5. Assign and discuss Exercises A and C on pages 265 and 266. You may prefer to do Exercise B as a class exercise.

Optional Practice Ask students to give the present (both forms), past, and future tense for all verbs in Exercise C on page 266. When discussing them, have students use them in sentences.

Extending the Lesson Ask students to design crossword puzzles that require knowledge of verb tenses for completion. Example:

a	t	e
	h	
	i	
	n	
	k	

Across
1. past tense of *eat*

Down
2. present tense of *thought*

Sentence Patterns The N V N Pattern p. 267

Objective To recognize the basic word order in sentences of the N V N sentence pattern

Presenting the Lesson 1. All three of these Sentence Pattern pages may be used at this time, or reserved for later review of verbs.

2. Read and discuss page 267. Make it clear that each of the

three parts in the N V N pattern may have one or more than one word. Any words that describe the subject noun are grouped in the first noun-part. Any words that describe the verb are grouped in the verb-part. Any words that describe the object noun are grouped in the second noun-part.

3. Assign and discuss Exercises A, B, and C. It may be useful to write examples for Exercise C on the board.

Extending the Lesson Point out that often an N V pattern sentence can be changed to an N V N pattern sentence by adding a single word, the direct object.

N V He ate.
N V N He ate lunch.

Have students write five pairs of sentences like those in the example. Use the words listed below:

won wrote plays sang called

Sentence Patterns The N LV N Pattern p. 268

Objective To recognize the basic word order in the N LV N sentence pattern

Presenting the Lesson 1. Read and discuss page 268. Make it clear that, as with the N V and N V N patterns, each part of an N LV N sentence may have one or more than one word.

2. Assign and discuss Exercises A, B, and C on page 268. It may be helpful to write examples of N LV N sentences from Exercise C on the board for examination.

Sentence Patterns The N LV Adj Pattern p. 269

Objective To recognize the use of adjectives in the N LV Adj sentence pattern

Presenting the Lesson 1. Read and discuss page 269. Avoid a thorough discussion of adjectives until Section 8 has been presented. Students should be able to discriminate between naming words—nouns—and describing words—adjectives—following a linking verb. If students raise the question, let them know there may be more than one word in the adjective-part of an N LV Adj sentence:

N	LV	Adj
Peter	is	very friendly.

2. Assign and discuss Exercises A, B, and C.

Extending the Lesson Which of the sentences below fits the N LV Adj pattern? Which sentences fit the patterns previously studied (N V, N V N, N LV N)?

1. She is friendly.
2. Lions roared.
3. Those pirates buried the treasure.
4. The children seem busy.
5. Kittens are cute baby animals.

Review

p. 270

You may use the review on page 270 either as a checkup or additional practice.

HANDBOOK SECTION 5

Using Irregular Verbs

Page 271-289

Objectives

1. To understand the function of the principal parts of verbs
2. To form the principal parts of regular verbs
3. To differentiate between regular and irregular verbs
4. To use the appropriate helping verb with the past participle
5. To use a dictionary to find principal parts of verbs
6. To recognize the principal parts of common irregular verbs
7. To use the principal parts of common irregular verbs correctly

Preparing the Students

Ask students to identify which word is used incorrectly in three of these sentences:

The children work problems.
The children work problems last month.
The children work problems next week.
The children should have work problems.

Writing the sentences on the board may help students see that the main verb should change its form to fit the time sentence.

If necessary, review verb tenses. See both the student material and the Teachers's Manual suggestions for Section 4, Part 5.

Part 1 Principal Parts of Verbs

Pages 271-272

Objective To understand the function of the principal parts of verbs

Presenting the Lesson 1. Read and discuss pages 271 and 272. Have students practice using the principal parts of the verbs listed at the top of the page 271 in sentences. Make sure that the students realize that the only difference between the past and past participle forms of regular verbs is the use of helping verbs with the past participle.

2. Remind students that as early learners of the language, children often use the regular form for all verbs, even when it might not be appropriate: *goed, runned, bringed.* This indicates how common the regular form is.

Optional Practice Have students identify form in each of these sentences:

1. Mark always dreaded spelling tests.
2. We have all learned that song.
3. Will you visit us next month?
4. Shelly's piano teacher plays beautifully.
5. The rabbit disappeared from the magician's hat.
6. That car has already been repaired.
7. The soldiers will attack at dawn.
8. I had completed the assignment early.
9. David bats third in today's line-up.
10. Which students created the best science project?

Part 2 **Regular Verbs** pp. 272-273

Objective To form the principal parts of regular verbs

Presenting the Lesson 1. Read and discuss page 272.
2. Assign and discuss Exercises A and B on page 273. Have students put some examples of correct sentences for Exercise B on the board and stress their use of helping verbs with the past participle.

Optional Practices Have students make three-column charts giving the principal parts of the following verbs: *play, cook, joke, wait, collect.*

Part 3 **Irregular Verbs** pp. 273-275

Objectives 1. To differentiate between regular and irregular verbs
2. To use the appropriate helping verb with the past participle
3. To use a dictionary to find principal parts of verbs
4. To recognize the principal parts of common irregular verbs

Presenting the Lesson 1. Read and discuss page 273. Be sure that students have a clear understanding of the difference between regular and irregular verbs.
2. Read Helping Verbs on page 274. Ask students for sentences using each listed form correctly. Stress the need for helping verbs with *be, been,* and *being.*
3. Read Using a Dictionary To Find Principal Parts, on page 274. If students have access to dictionaries, have them look up these irregular verbs: *think, drive, build.*
4. Students should learn the forms of the common irregular verbs on page 275.

Optional Practice Have students use dictionaries to locate and list the principal parts of the following verbs:

lend	sink	catch
tear	bite	swing
creep	draw	wake
eat	grow	steal
lie	draw	make
lay	feel	break

Part 4 Practice Pages on Irregular Verbs

pp. 276-228

Objective To practice the correct use of irregular verbs

Presenting the Lesson 1. Have students read the explanatory paragraphs on page 276.

2. Administer the diagnostic test (Exercise) on page 276.

3. Assign individual work on the practice pages 277-288, based on each student's weaknesses on the diagnostic test. In this list, the number in parentheses following each verb refers to the test item on that verb.

come/came/come	(3)	see/saw/seen	(12)
do/did/done	(4,5)	speak/spoke/spoken	(7)
drink/drank/drunk	(1,14)	swim/swam/swum	(10)
fall/fell/fallen	(2)	take/took/taken	(13)
give/gave/given	(8)	write/wrote/written	(15)
go/went/gone	(9)		
run/ran/run	(6,11)		

4. Develop each of the practice pages separately. They should not be presented as an uninterrupted unit.

On each practice page, have the students read and compare the sentences in Say It Right, Hear It Right until they can develop rules for using the forms of that verb, such as these:

Use *went* by itself.

Use *gone* with a helping verb.

When they show this ability, assign the exercise entitled Write It Right. Reinforce the lesson by having the students correct their papers together.

Optional Practice Do a class oral activity with the words on page 275. Have the students take turns creating sentences with each of the principal parts of each irregular verb. Discuss any errors.

Extending the Lesson Can students think of other irregular verbs to add to the list on page 275. What are the principal parts?

Review

p. 289

You may use the review on page 289 either as a checkup or for additional practice.

Using Troublesome Verbs Correctly

Pages 290-301

Objectives

1. To choose the correct verb from verb pairs that are often confused
2. To use negative words correctly
3. To form good speech habits regarding some commonly misused verb forms

Preparing the Students

Read page 290. Then list the following phrases on the board:

Lay down.—Lie down.
don't do nothing—don't do anything
aren't—ain't

Point out that all of these phrases are heard in conversation. However, some of them are not always used correctly. Others may be accepted in a casual conversation but do not belong in a formal discussion, such as a job interview. Many people have difficulty deciding when it is correct to use phrases such as these. This section will give the students practice in using such confusing words correctly.

Part 1 Pairs of Verbs That Are Often Confused

pp. 291-297

Objective To choose the correct verb from verb pairs that are often confused.

Presenting the Lesson 1. This Part discusses six pairs of verbs, and provides an exercise for each pair and Review Exercises after each group of three. It is recommended that each pair be covered in a separate lesson, perhaps in conjunction with other review or enrichment material, so that each section gets individual attention. If you use this approach, assign the Exercises as suggested in the following steps.

If you prefer, you may present this Part in only two units: the first set of three verb pairs (through the Review Exercises on pages 293 and 294); and the second set of three verb pairs (through the Review Exercises on pages 296 and 297). If you use this approach, it is recommended that you do orally the Exercises in steps 3, 5, 7, 10, 12, and 14. Assign only the Review Exercises (steps 8 and 15) to be written.

2. Read and discuss page 291. Discuss the right meaning of the examples and the wrong meaning that occurs with the wrong choice.

3. Assign and discuss the Exercise on page 291.

4. Read and discuss Leave and Let on page 292.

5. Assign and discuss the Exercise on page 292.

6. Read and discuss Lie and Lay on page 292. Students are unlikely to confuse *lie* in the sense of telling an untruth, with *lay*.

7. Assign and discuss the Exercise at the top of page 293.

8. Assign and discuss Review Exercises A and B on pages 293 and 294.

9. Read and discuss page 294.

10. Assign and discuss the Exercise on pages 294 and 295.

11. Read and discuss Sit and Set on page 295.

12. Assign and discuss the Exercise on page 295.

13. Read and discuss Teach and Learn on page 295.

14. Assign and discuss the Exercise at the top of page 296.

15. Assign and discuss Review Exercises A and B on pages 296 and 297.

Part 2 **Using Negatives Correctly** pp. 297-299

Objective To use negatives correctly in sentences

Presenting the Lesson 1. Read and discuss pages 297 and 298.

2. Explain that in some sentences two negatives cancel each other out. If "He does *not* have *no* paper," then he does have paper. Usually a speaker using a double negative means to emphasize the negative. Point out that the meaning is much clearer when only one negative is used.

3. Assign roles and do Exercise A on page 298 aloud. Assign and discuss Exercise B.

Optional Practice Have students choose the correct word from the parentheses.

1. The stranger won't tell (anybody, nobody) his name.
2. Meg has done (anything/nothing) about the cookie drive.
3. Couldn't you see (nothing/anything)?
4. Don't you have (none/any) of those green ribbons?
5. Doesn't the bakery have (any more, no more) bread?
6. Can't (nobody, anybody) open that window?
7. Didn't you win (nothing, anything)?
8. Thunder doesn't hurt (anyone, no one).

Part 3 Good Speech Habits

pp. 299-300

Objective To form good speech habits regarding some commonly misused verb forms

Presenting the Lesson 1. Read and discuss page 299. Point out that what is accepted in casual conversation is not always accepted in more formal situations. It is helpful to develop good habits by using the approved form as often as possible, including casual conversations.

2. It is suggested that Exercise A on pages 299 and 300 be done aloud. Assign and discuss Exercise B.

Optional Practice Ask students to match as many correct pronoun-verb or noun-verb combinations as they can from these two columns.

I	am not
you	isn't
he	aren't
she	haven't
it	hasn't
we	don't
they	doesn't
the cat	was
Ruby and Lee	weren't

Review

p. 301

You may use the review on page 301 either as a checkup or additional practice.

Using Pronouns

Pages 302-312

Objectives

1. To understand the concept of the pronoun
2. To recognize the singular and plural personal pronouns
3. To use pronouns correctly as subjects of sentences, particularly in compound subjects
4. To use pronouns correctly after linking verbs
5. To use pronouns correctly as objects in sentences, particularly in compound objects
6. To recognize and use the possessive pronouns
7. To distinguish between the possessive pronoun *its* and the contraction *it's*

Preparing the Students

Write this sentence on the board.

The girl is holding the cup.

Cross out the words *The girl* and ask for one word, not a name, that can be used in place of *The girl. (She)* Then cross out the words *the cup* and ask for one word to replace the phrase. *(It)*

Point out that the sentence *She is holding it* is not clear by itself. It makes sense only when everyone knows who *she* and *it* stand for. Explain that *she* and *it* are called pronouns, and will be discussed with other pronouns in this section.

Part 1 What Are Pronouns?

pp. 302-304

Objectives 1. To understand the concept of the pronoun

2. To recognize the singular and plural personal pronouns

Presenting the Lesson 1. Read and discuss pages 302 and 303. Give special attention to the three uses of pronouns.

2. As an oral exercise, have students practice using each of the pronouns on page 303 in sentences.

3. Assign and discuss Exercises A and B on page 304.

Optional Practice Ask students to rewrite the following paragraph, using pronouns in place of overused nouns.

> Sharon wrote a story about Sharon's cat. Sharon took the story to school. Sharon hoped that Sharon's teacher would like the story and would give Sharon an A.

Extending the Lesson Ask students to bring short newspaper articles to class. Have them underline all of the pronouns in the article. On a separate sheet of paper they should then list every underlined pronoun and the noun that it stands for.

Part 2 Pronouns in Subjects

pp. 305-306

Objective To use pronouns correctly as subjects of sentences, particularly in compound subjects

Presenting the Lesson 1. Review the construction of complete sentences (subject plus predicate). Point out that in the sentences studied thus far, the subjects have been nouns. Pronouns, as substitutes for nouns, may take over the job of the subject.

2. Read and discuss pages 305 and 306. Stress that the pronoun that is correct in a simple subject is also correct in a compound subject. Have students refer to the pronoun list on page 303, and try each pronoun by itself as the subject of a sentence. The students should have no trouble accepting the rule listing which pronouns should be used as subjects and which should not.

3. It is suggested that you do Exercise A on page 306 orally with the class. Encourage students to listen to the sound of the pronoun in the sentence. Assign and discuss Exercise B.

Optional Practice Ask students to identify the subject of each sentence below. Then have them rewrite each sentence, substituting a pronoun for each subject.

1. The wooden fence blew down in the windstorm
2. Two friendly police officers gave directions.
3. The talented actress won an Oscar
4. My little brother lost his bicycle.
5. Nancy and Marty climbed Mt. Evans last summer.

Part 3 **Pronouns After Linking Verbs** pp. 307-308

Objective To use pronouns correctly after linking verbs

Presenting the Lesson 1. Review the definition of linking verbs as discussed in Section 4.

2. Read and discuss page 307. Because they are interchangeable, the pronoun following a linking verb must be able to sound right when used as a subject. Stress the sound of the pronoun when used as a subject to ensure the correct pronoun choice. Most students are not comfortable with the sound of the correct pronoun choice following a linking verb.

3. It is recommended that you do Exercise A on pages 307 and 308 with the class. After each sentence, ask students to exchange the subject noun or pronoun with the predicate noun or pronoun. Assign and discuss Exercise B.

Optional Practice Ask students to identify the nouns following each of these linking verbs. Have them rewrite each sentence, substituting pronouns for these nouns.

1. The wooden fence blew down in the windstorm.
2. Two friendly police officers gave directions.
3. The talented actress won an Oscar.
4. My little brother lost his bicycle.
5. The runners are Brian and Wally.

Part 4 **Pronouns as Objects** pp. 308-309

Objective To use pronouns correctly as objects in sentences, particularly in compound objects

Presenting the Lesson 1. Review Part 3 in Section 4 (action verbs and direct objects).

2. Read and discuss pages 308 and 309. Have the students refer once more to the pronouns listed on page 303, and try each one by itself as the object of a verb. Most students will naturally approve of each correct object pronoun by the way it sounds in the sentence.

3. It is suggested that Exercise A on page 309 be done as a class activity. Assign and discuss Exercise B on page 310.

Optional Practice Many students will insist on the incorrect pronoun choice *I* when selecting the first pronoun used in a compound object. *Me* somehow seems less formal. Emphasize the choice of pronouns in a compound by the choice of each one separately. Few students who insist on "They chose he and I" will like the sound of "They chose I." Ask the students for original sentences using *me* correctly.

Part 5 Possessive Pronouns

pp. 310-311

Objectives 1. To recognize and use the possessive pronouns

2. To distinguish between the possessive pronoun *its* and the contraction *it's*

Presenting the Lesson 1. Write this sentence on the board:

Here is Amy's sweater.

Ask students to identify the possessive noun. It may be necessary to review Section 3, Part 4, on possessive nouns. Ask students if they can suggest a pronoun to use in place of the noun.

2. Read and discuss pages 310 and 311.

3. It may be helpful to do Exercise A on page 311 as a class activity. Assign and discuss Exercise B. For Exercise B, stress that each time a student adds an apostrophe, he or she should test the answer by substituting *it is* for *it's*. If the substitution does not fit, the answer is incorrect.

Optional Practice Rewrite the following sentences, substituting possessive pronouns for the possessive nouns.

1. Ms. Walker's class is very busy.
2. Barry's hair is bright red.
3. The girls' pictures were in the newspaper.
4. The rabbit's leg was broken.

Review

p. 312

You may use the review on page 312 either as a checkup or for additional practice.

Using Adjectives

Pages 313-326

Objectives

1. To understand the function of the adjective, and to identify adjectives in sentences
2. To identify and use articles
3. To understand the function of predicate adjectives, and to use predicate adjectives
4. To recognize the formation of proper adjectives, and to use proper adjectives with correct capitalization
5. To use the demonstrative adjectives *(this, that, these, those)* correctly
6. To differentiate between *those,* used as either a demonstrative adjective or pronoun, and *them,* used only as a pronoun
7. To form the comparative and superlative forms of adjectives, and to choose the correct form in sentences

Preparing the Students

Using either the word "boy" or the word "girl," add adjectives to describe a particular student in the room until everyone can guess the person's identity. (e.g., boy; tall boy; tall, blonde boy; tall, blonde, muscular boy; tall, blonde, muscular, brown-eyed boy) Explain that the descriptive words you kept adding are adjectives, which help to make descriptions more specific, and that their use will be further explored in this chapter.

Part 1 What Are Adjectives?

pp. 313-316

Objective To understand the function of the adjective, and to identify adjectives in sentences

Presenting the Lesson 1. Read and discuss the introduction to Part 1 on pages 313 and 314. Make sure the students are conscious of how the meaning of the sentences at the top of page 314 changes with the substitution of different adjectives. How many more adjectives can students think of to fit the basic sentence?

2. Read Some Adjectives Tell *What Kind.* Ask students to change the meaning of the five sample sentences by changing the adjectives in italics. Note the adjective endings listed at the bottom of the page. Can students think of additional adjectives with these endings?

3. Read Some Adjectives Tell *How Many.* Discuss how the four sample sentences can be changed by changing the adjectives in italics. Point out that adjectives can tell "how many" in countable amounts (one, sixteen) or in general amounts (few, several).

4. Read Some Adjectives Tell *Which Ones.* Point out that these adjectives do not describe the nouns they modify, but serve to point them out. Specific information on demonstrative adjectives, and practice in their use, will be presented in Part 5 of this section. At this time it should not be necessary to go into detail.

5. In addition to the definition of an adjective presented in Section 8, there are other ways to identify an adjective. These ways, listed in the following chart, are based on what linguists have discovered about the structure of a word and the order of words in a sentence. It is suggested that the information in the chart be used to point out additional ways in which adjectives function.

Ways To Identify Adjectives

1. Adjectives have more than one form. They change form to show comparison. Adjectives of more than two syllables usually show comparison by using the words *more* and *most.*

bright	brighter	brightest
good	better	best
beautiful	more beautiful	most beautiful

2. Adjectives are often preceded by words such as *very, quite,* or *much.*

   very bright   quite good   much better

3. Adjectives usually occur before nouns.

   Rosa has a *beautiful* ring.
   Juan has the *best* idea.

6. It is suggested that you do both Exercises A and B on page 316 with the class.

Optional Practice Ask students to supply three different adjectives to modify each of the following nouns. Write a sentence using each noun with one of the adjectives.

dress	flowers	lawn
table	dinner	horse

Part 2 The Article pp. 317-318

Objective To identify and use articles

Presenting the Lesson 1. Read aloud The Articles on page 317. Point out that *the* can be used with either beginning consonant or vowel sounds. If students bring up the question, explain that the long *u* sound is grouped with the consonants. The article *a* is used before the long *u* sound. (*a* uniform, not *an* uniform)

2. Point out that articles are special adjectives that specify nouns but do not describe them. They are never used with pronouns.

3. It is suggested that Exercise A on page 317 be done orally. Assign and discuss Exercise B on page 318.

Optional Practice Decide whether *a* or *an* should be used with each of the following words or phrases.

_______ box	_______ unusual test
_______ eggplant	_______ hourglass
_______ jar	_______ ill friend
_______ old recipe	_______ plate
_______ thick shake	_______ average score

Extending the Lesson Explain that the article *the* is called a definite article because it specifies a particular item.

the envelope (a specific envelope)
the book (a specific book)

A and *an* are indefinite articles because they do not indicate a specific item.

an envelope (any one)
a book (any one)

Ask students to identify each article they used in Exercise B as definite or indefinite.

Part 3 Predicate Adjectives

pp. 318-319

Objective To understand the function of predicate adjectives, and to use predicate adjectives

Presenting the Lesson 1. Briefly review linking verbs (Section 4, Part 4). Remind students that linking verbs connect the subject with a word in the predicate.

2. Read Predicate Adjectives on page 318. Be sure that students understand that the adjective in the predicate must modify the subject, and not any other noun. Here is a sample sentence:

The flower is a yellow daisy.

The adjective *yellow* modifies the noun *daisy* and not the subject *flower. Yellow* is not a predicate adjective. Here is another sentence:

The flower is yellow.

The adjective *yellow* modifies the subject *flower.* In this sentence, *yellow* is a predicate adjective.

3. It is suggested that you do Exercise A, on pages 318 and 319, with the class. Assign and discuss Exercise B.

Optional Practice Have the students tell whether the italicized adjective is a predicate adjective. If it does not modify the subject, what noun does it modify?

1. My favorite sweater is *beige.*
2. The dog was a *gray* poodle.
3. Bill's uncle is *friendly.*
4. The explorers were *restless* travelers.
5. Several parents were *present.*

Part 4 Proper Adjectives

pp. 319-320

Objective To recognize the formation of proper adjectives, and to use proper adjectives with correct capitalization

Presenting the Lesson 1. Review proper nouns (Section 3, Part 2). Emphasize that all proper nouns are capitalized. (Be sure that students do not confuse the words *proper nouns* with the word *pronouns.*)

2. Read pages 319 and 320. Ask students for examples of both

types of proper adjectives: those formed by adding adjective endings to proper nouns, and those formed by using proper nouns in adjective positions.

3. Assign and discuss Exercises A and B on page 320.

Extending the Lesson 1. What is the proper adjective that corresponds with each of the following proper nouns?

Alaska	Wales	Canada
America	Ireland	France

2. Use each of the words below in two sentences: first, as a proper noun, and then as a proper adjective.

Muppet   Chevrolet   Dr. Seuss

Part 5 Demonstrative Adjectives

pp. 321-323

Objectives 1. To use the demonstrative adjectives *(this, that, these, those)* correctly

2. To differentiate between *those,* used as either a demonstrative adjective or pronoun, and *them,* used only as a pronoun

Presenting the Lesson 1. Read pages 321 and 322. Ask students to suggest phrases using the four demonstratives. Make sure the students realize that *this* and *that* modify nouns that are close at hand, while *these* and *those* refer to nouns that are at a distance.

2. Some students will need more emphasis on the *them/those* usage than others. Plan the discussion to suit the needs of your class.

3. It is suggested that you do Exercises A and B on pages 322 and 323 as a class activity. What are the common errors?

Optional Practice Ask students to add a demonstrative adjective to each sentence below. They should be able to tell whether the modified noun is singular or plural.

1. ______ birthday card will make her happy.
2. Can you bring ______ paper with you?
3. ______ trees are covered with apple blossoms.
4. I read ______ books.
5. Did you find ______ dictionary?

Extending the Lesson Discuss the difference between the use of demonstratives as adjectives and their use as pronouns. As adjectives they must modify nouns. Have students decide whether each of the underlined words is a demonstrative adjective or a demonstrative pronoun, and give reasons for their answers.

1. *This* is very important.
2. *These* answers are correct.
3. *That* is not funny.
4. *That* cheerleader is full of school spirit.

Part 6 Making Comparisons with Adjectives

pp. 323-325

Objective To form the comparative and superlative forms of adjectives, and to choose the correct form in sentences

Presenting the Lesson 1. Read pages 323 and 324. Make sure the students see the difference between the comparative form (used to compare two things) and the superlative form (used to compare three or more things).

2. Point out that long adjectives would be difficult to pronounce with *er* or *est* added. It is easier to say and understand a long adjective with *more* or *most* before it.

3. Ask students to suggest sentences using the comparative and superlative forms of *good* and *bad*. Can students give both forms for these adjectives:

little (less, least, or littler, littlest) many (more, most)
much (more, most) ill (worse, worst)

Tell students that the dictionary will provide comparative and superlative forms of adjectives that do not follow the regular patterns.

4. Point out that only adjectives that describe (tell *what kind*) can be used in comparisons. Demonstratives, articles, proper adjectives, and adjectives that tell *how many* do not have forms for comparison.

5. It is suggested that you do Exercise A on page 325 orally. Discuss reasons for each answer. Assign and discuss Exercise B.

Review

p. 326

You may use the review on page 326 either as a checkup or for additional practice.

Using Adverbs

Pages 327-336

Objectives

1. To understand the function of the adverb, and to identify adverbs in sentences
2. To form the comparative and superlative forms of adverbs, and to use the correct form in sentences
3. To differentiate between adverbs and adjectives, and to make the correct choice in sentences

Preparing the Students

Remind the students that they learned in Section 8 how adjectives can modify nouns. Then explain that this Section will present another group of words that can be used to describe words other than nouns and their substitutes, pronouns.

Part 1 What Are Adverbs?

pp. 327-330

Objective To understand the function of the adverb, and to identify adverbs in sentences

Presenting the Lesson 1. Read pages 327 to 329. Discuss the sentences in the examples. Can students offer other adverbs for each example?

2. Ask students to form adverbs by adding *-ly* to the adjectives in this list:

sure	fair	warm
loud	correct	new

3. In addition to the definition of an adverb given in Section 9, there are other ways to identify an adverb, based on what linguists have discovered about the structure of a word and the order of words in a sentence. The following chart lists these ways. It is suggested that the information in the chart be used to point out additional ways in which adverbs function.

Ways To Identify Adverbs

1. Adverbs are often difficult to separate from adjectives. One of the best ways to identify adverbs is by their positions in sentences. They are most often found at the end of a sentence.

    She plays *well.*
    He moves *fast.*

2. Adverbs can also be found in other places in a sentence.

    At the Beginning
        Now I will hurry.
    Between Subject and Verb
        The people *here* are honest.
    Within Verb Phrases
        You can *sometimes* see the tower.
    Before an Adjective
        David was *unusually* quiet.

3. Look for words that fit the blank in this test sentence:
    He did it________.

4. Look for words with the ending *-ly:*
    adjective + *ly* = adverb
    bad + ly = badly
    quickly + ly = quickly

4. It is suggested that Exercise A on page 329 be done together. Assign and discuss Exercises B and C on pages 329 and 330.

Optional Practice Have students use each of the adverbs in Exercise A in original sentences. Discuss what words they modify. Are they verbs, adjectives, or other adverbs?

Extending the Lesson 1. Have students try their hands at creating "Tom Swifties." Follow the pattern of these examples.

"The ocean is very choppy," said Tom roughly.
"Turn on the light," she said brightly.
"Would you like a cold drink?" he asked icily.

2. Present the chart Ways to Identify Adverbs. Discuss the four sentence positions in which adverbs may appear. Ask students for examples of each.

It is important to point out that not every adverb can be placed in all four of these positions. The structure of the sentence must be considered. Students should let the sound of the sentence be their guide when positioning adverbs.

Ask the students to rewrite each of these sentences by placing the adverb in a different position.

The cat purred *softly.*
Quickly my sister ran home.
That saw is *loudly* buzzing.

Part 2 Making Comparisons with Adverbs
pp. 330-332

Objective To form comparative and superlative forms of adverbs, and to use the correct form in sentences

Presenting the Lesson 1. Read pages 330 and 331. Discuss the similarities between the adjective and adverb forms of comparison.

2. Assign and discuss Exercises A and B on pages 331 and 332.

Optional Practice Use each of the words in Exercise A on page 331 in a sentence. Identify whether the adverbs tell *how, when, where,* or *to what extent.*

Part 3 Adjective or Adverb? pp. 332-335

Objective To differentiate between adverbs and adjectives, and to make the correct choice in sentences

Presenting the Lesson 1. Read and discuss the first section of Part 3, page 332 and 333. Place particular emphasis on the different questions answered by adjectives and adverbs.

2. Use these sentences for practice. Ask students to fill in the blanks, and to tell whether the word supplied is an adjective or an adverb. The students should be able to tell which word is being modified.

1. That music is________loud.
2. Jogging is________than running.

3. Please find the answer_________.
4. She_________raised her hand.
5. The swallow flew away_________.

3. It is suggested that you do Exercise A on page 333 with the class. Assign and discuss Exercise B on page 334.

4. Read Using Good and Well on pages 334 and 335. Make sure the students understand the meaning and use of each word. Use the following sentences for practice. Ask students to choose the correct word in parentheses. They should be able to identify the word being modified.

1. That is a (good, well) answer.
2. The skater performed (good, well) at the Olympics.
3. After eating the third candy bar, I don't feel so (good, well).
4. Their dog is a (good, well) hunter.
5. That band played (good, well).

5. It is suggested that Exercise A on page 335 be done as a class activity. Assign and discuss Exercise B.

Optional Practice Point out that when *well* is used as an adjective to describe a state of health (*I feel well*), the verb in such sentences is a linking verb. Only linking verbs are followed by predicate adjectives.

Decide whether the verb in each sentence below is an action verb or a linking verb. Tell if *well* is used as an adjective or an adverb.

1. The trained seal performed well.
2. I don't feel too well.
3. She dresses well.
4. She seems well today.
5. The athlete ran well today.

Review

p. 336

You may use the review on page 336 either as a checkup or for additional practice.

Using Prepositions and Conjunctions

Pages 337-351

Objectives

1. To understand the function of the preposition, and to identify prepositions and prepositional phrases in sentences
2. To identify nouns and pronouns as objects of prepositions, and to use the correct pronoun forms as objects of prepositions
3. To differentiate between the use of a word as a preposition and its use as an adverb
4. To identify prepositional phrases as adjective or adverb phrases
5. To avoid confusion caused by misplaced prepositional phrases
6. To understand the function of the conjunction

Preparing the Students

Ask the students to recall the parts of speech they have already studied: nouns, verbs, pronouns, adjectives, and adverbs. Explain that there are two parts of speech, prepositions and conjunctions, which are used to connect and relate other words and ideas in a sentence. These words showing relationships will be studied in this section. Read the introduction to Section 10 on page 337.

Part 1 What Are Prepositions?

pp. 338-341

Objective To understand the function of the preposition, and to identify prepositions and prepositional phrases in sentences

Presenting the Lesson 1. Read and discuss pages 338 and 339. Can students suggest other ways to change the sample sentences? Make sure the students realize the difference between a *preposition* and a *prepositional phrase.*

2. As a class exercise, have students take turns making up sentences with the words in the lists at the top of page 339. Be sure

that they use the words as prepositions and not as adverbs.

3. Assign and discuss the Exercise on page 339.

4. Read and discuss Using Prepositional Phrases on page 340. Emphasize that the prepositional phrase must be at least two words, but may be more. You may wish to point out that the question *what?* may be used to find the object of the preposition, just as it was to find the direct object of the verb.

5. Assign and discuss Exercises A and B on pages 340 and 341.

Optional Practice 1. Ask students to copy each of the following sentences and label each word according to its part of speech.

1. That clock rang early in the morning.
2. We ran around a track.
3. My dog chased after a rabbit.
4. The sandwich was on the plate.
5. I like days without rain.

2. Play a game of Prepositional Phrase Charades. Make a set of cards with a prepositional phrase on each. One student draws a card and acts out the phrase. No talking is allowed. The first student to identify the phrase correctly gets the next turn.

Example phrases: under the desk
beside the table
in the doorway

Extending the Lesson Have each student bring to class a magazine or newspaper ad that contains one or more prepositional phrases (the more the better). Ask them to circle each phrase. They should be prepared to present their findings to the class. The ads can then be used to create an interesting "real world" bulletin board display.

Part 2 Objects of Prepositions

pp. 341-344

Objective To identify nouns and pronouns as objects of prepositions, and to use the correct pronoun forms as objects of prepositions.

Presenting the Lesson 1. Read and discuss page 341. Remind the students that asking *what?* after the preposition helps to identify its object.

2. It is suggested that you do the Exercise on page 341 orally.

3. Remind students that pronouns are substitutes for nouns, so objects of prepositions can be nouns or pronouns. Read Using Pronouns as Objects of Prepositions and discuss how sentences in the preceding exercise could be changed by substituting a pronoun for each noun object.

4. Read Using Pronouns in Compound Objects of Prepositions on page 342. Remind the class that *compound* means "more than one." Stress the choice of pronouns in compounds by first considering the pronoun as a single object. Carefully discuss the sample sentences.

5. Read Using *Between* and *Among*. Make sure that students understand the difference in their use. For practice, ask students to decide whether each of the following sentences is correct as is, or if it needs to be corrected.

1. They had to choose among pie or ice cream.
2. That is a problem between all the nations of the world.
3. What is the difference between this one and that one?
4. We will divide the candy among all six boys.

6. It is suggested that Exercise A on page 343 be done orally. Assign and discuss Exercise B on pages 343 and 344.

Part 3 Preposition or Adverb? pp. 344-345

Objective To differentiate between the use of a word as a preposition and its use as an adverb.

Presenting the Lesson 1. Review the definition and function of adverbs in Section 9.

2. Read and discuss page 344. Stress that a preposition must be followed by an object (noun or pronoun). Prepositions must be part of a phrase.

3. You may prefer to do Exercise A on pages 344 and 345 as a class activity. Students should be able to explain reasons for each answer. Assign and discuss Exercise B on page 345.

Optional Practice Use each of the following words in two sentences, first as a preposition, and second as an adverb.

under	by	off
above	across	in

Part 4 Prepositional Phrases as Modifiers

pp. 346-347

Objective To identify prepositional phrases as adjective or adverb phrases

Presenting the Lesson 1. Read and discuss page 346. Stress that prepositional phrases function just as adjectives and adverbs do, in terms of modifying nouns, pronouns, and verbs.

2. It is recommended that Exercise A on pages 346 and 347 be done as a class activity. Assign and discuss Exercise B.

Extending the Lesson Ask students to write two sentences with each of the following phrases, using it first as an adjective phrase and then as an adverb phrase.

in the house
with my sister
across the street
on my head
between those buildings

Part 5 Using Prepositional Phrases in the Right Places

pp. 347-349

Objective To avoid confusion caused by misplaced prepositional phrases

Presenting the Lesson 1. Read and discuss pages 347 and 348. Make sure students are conscious of the difference in meaning between the two forms of the second example.

2. It is suggested that you do Exercise A on page 348 with the class. Ask students to tell how the meaning of the sentence changes with the change in word order. Assign and discuss Exercise B on pages 348 and 349.

Optional Practice Have students change the word order in each of the following sentences, to clarify the meaning.

1. Sharon hung the clock over the table with the loud chime.
2. A flock of geese flew over our heads on their way south.
3. Jason whistled for the cat with the food bowl in his hand.
4. The car limped to the gas station with a flat tire.

Part 6 What Are Conjunctions?

pp. 349-350

Objective To understand the function of the conjunction

Presenting the Lesson 1. Read and discuss pages 349 and 350. Analyze each of the six sentences showing various sentence parts that can be combined by conjunctions. Make sure the students can identify the words being connected by the italicized conjunction, and the role of those words in the sentence.

2. Students who have mastered the parts of sentences studied thus far should have little difficulty with the various kinds of compound structures shown on pages 349 and 350. Some students, however, may have difficulty understanding these compounds. Such students should review sentence parts studied in previous chapters, and should be asked only to identify conjunctions in sectences. They should not be required to write compound sentences, and sentences with compound parts, at this time.

3. It is recommended that the class do Exercise A on page 350 as an oral exercise. Assign Exercise B only to those students who showed competence on Exercise A. Discuss Exercise B when it is completed. Students who had difficulty with Exercise A should do the Optional Practice Exercise in place of Exercise B.

Optional Practice In the sentences below, one part is italicized. Have the students tell whether the italicized part is a compound subject, a compound predicate, or a compound object. They must also identify the conjunction.

1. *Singers and dancers* auditioned for the musical.
2. The car *needs repairs but still runs.*
3. Phyllis *repaired her vase and the old pitcher.*
4. Henry wanted *a mystery or an adventure story.*
5. I *wrote a letter but need a stamp.*
6. *Iced tea or lemonade* tastes good on a hot day.

Review

p.351

You may use the review on page 351 either as a checkup or for additional practice.

The Parts of Speech

Pages 352-357

Objectives

1. To understand the function of the interjection
2. To review the eight parts of speech
3. To recognize the use of a single word as various parts of speech

Preparing the Students

Ask students to name all the types of words studied so far. Ask them how to identify a noun (verb, pronoun, etc.) and what job that type of word does. Point out that all these different kinds of words are needed to help us express our ideas to other people.

Part 1 The Parts of Speech

pp. 352-354

Objectives 1. To understand the function of the interjection
2. To review the eight parts of speech

Presenting the Lesson 1. Read and discuss the material on pages 352 and 353. It might be helpful to use the Optional Practice exercises below as an oral review activity at this time.

2. Assign and discuss Exercises A and B on pages 353 and 354.

Optional Practice Using the following sentences, have the students identify which part of speech each word is. Ask them to list the words in four columns, headed *Nouns, Verbs, Adjectives,* and *Adverbs.*

1. Dogs can often understand many words.
2. Usually Reuben finishes these chores quickly.
3. Later Gloria will serve cherry pie.
4. This tire needs some air.
5. The girls will probably take the bus.

2. Have the students find the pronouns, prepositions, conjunctions, and interjections in the following sentences.

1. The winners of the poster contest were Jim and I.
2. You should wear a jacket or a heavy sweater to the game.
3. Quick! Throw him that life preserver!
4. Wind and rain blew into the tent through holes in the canvas.
5. Ouch! You stepped on my foot.

Part 2 Using Words as Different Parts of Speech

pp. 354-356

Objective To recognize the use of a single word as different parts of speech

Presenting the Lesson 1. Read and discuss the material on pages 354 and 355, with particular attention to the sample sentences.

2. Encourage students to use a dictionary for examples of words used as more than one part of speech. Have them look especially for sample sentences in entries for such words.

3. It is suggested that Exercise A on pages 355 and 356 be done as a class activity. Assign and discuss Exercise B. Note that in B, 8, the italicized words have different pronunciations.

Optional Practice Use each word below in at least two different sentences, each time as a different part of speech.

picture	down	stone
cup	flower	paint
water	fish	ink

Review

p. 357

You may use the review on page 357 either as a checkup or for additional practice.

Making Subjects and Verbs Agree

Pages 358-369

Objectives

1. To become aware of the importance of subject and verb agreement
2. To be alert to certain difficult subjects in sentences, and to use the correct verb form with each of these subjects

Preparing the Students

Remind the students that in Handbook Section 3, Part 3, they learned that nouns have two forms, singular and plural. In Handbook Section 4, Part 5, they learned that verbs in the present tense also have two forms. Explain that this chapter will give more information about how these forms work together. It will help the students recognize some important speech patterns and apply them in their speech and writing.

Read and discuss page 358.

Part 1 Rules for Making the Subject and Verb Agree

pp. 359-362

Objective To become aware of the importance of subject and verb agreement

Presenting the Lesson 1. Read and discuss page 359, through the two rules. Emphasize the *s* ending as the mark of the singular form of most verbs. Let the students know that another term for "making the subject and verb agree" is *agreement of subject and verb.*

2. Read and discuss Prepositional Phrases After the Subject, on pages 359 and 360. (Note that understanding of this section is required in Exercise B.) Point out that it is helpful to read the sentence, leaving out the prepositional phrases; this should clearly indicate which word is the subject.

3. Assign and discuss Exercises A and B on pages 360 and 361. For Exercise B, suggest the students first identify any prepo-

sitional phrases in the complete subject, and then find the simple subject. It may also be helpful to develop Exercise A further as a class activity. Ask students to supply a possible verb that agrees with each subject. Use each subject and verb in a sentence.

4. Read page 361. Put the following chart on the board and discuss it.

	Singular	Plural
Present Tense	is has does	are have do
Past Tense	was had did	were had did

Discuss also the negative contractions of the words on the chart, such as *isn't* and *hasn't*. Ask the students which of the verbs and negative contractions may be used with *he, she, we,* and *they*. (Be sure students understand the purpose of the apostrophe.)

5. It is suggested that Exercise A on pages 361 and 362 be done orally. Assign and discuss Exercise B.

Optional Practice Have the students choose the correct verb form for each sentence.

1. Two cans of lemonade (is, are) not enough for everyone.
2. One of the teachers (is, are) coming with us on the field trip.
3. Many fish (live, lives) in this pond.
4. The horses in the corral (has, have) all been fed.
5. They (wasn't, weren't) at Carol's party last night.

Part 2 **Special Problems with Subjects** pp. 362-368

Objective To be alert to certain difficult subjects in sentences, and to use the correct verb form with each of these subjects

Presenting the Lesson 1. Read and discuss pages 362 and 363.

2. It is suggested that you do Exercise A on pages 363 and 364 as a class activity. Some students may need to review prepositional

phrases (Handbook Section 10). Point out that in the interrogative form (item 10), it is helpful to turn the question into a statement before determining subject and verb. Assign and discuss Exercise B on page 364.

3. Read and discuss page 364.
4. It is suggested that Exercise A on page 365 be done as a class activity. Assign and discuss Exercise B.
5. Read and discuss Compound Subjects on pages 365 and 366. Stress the difference between *and* and the other conjunctions used in a subject.
6. It is suggested that Exercise A on page 366 be done orally. Assign and discuss Exercise B on pages 366 and 367.
7. Read and discuss page 367.
8. Assign and discuss Exercise A and B on pages 367 and 368.

Extending the Lesson Tell the students that the pronouns listed on page 362 are called *indefinite pronouns*. Ask if they can explain that name.

Review

p. 369

You may use the review on page 369 either as a checkup or for additional practice.

HANDBOOK SECTION 13

Using Compound Sentences

Pages 370-377

Objectives

1. To review the parts of the simple sentence
2. To understand the definition of the compound sentence
3. To recognize the parts of compound sentences
4. To write compound sentences and to punctuate them correctly

Preparing the Students

Ask how many of the students like a certain popular dish, such as pizza. Then ask how many would like to eat nothing but that one dish for an entire month. Most of the class will agree that that would be too much of a good thing. Point out that most people like variety in everything—food, clothes, entertainment—and that good writing, too, needs variety. Remind the students that they have already learned much about sentences in Handbook Sections 1 and 2. In this section and the next, they will learn more about sentences in order to add variety to their writing.

Part 1 A Review of the Sentence pp. 370-372

Objective To review the parts of the simple sentence

Presenting the Lesson 1. Read and discuss pages 370 and 371. Make sure that the students can explain the definition of a simple sentence.

2. It is suggested that Exercise A on page 372 be done as a class activity. Assign and discuss Exercises B and C.

Extending the Lesson Have the students combine the sentences in each of the following sets to form a simple sentence with a compound subject or a compound predicate. They should eliminate or change words as necessary, but retain all the ideas in the original set.

1. Our school library has many books.
   Our library also provides a good selection of magazines.
2. Florida is known for its vacation spots.
   California is known for its vacation spots.
3. Ice hockey is a popular sport in Russia.
   Soccer is also a popular sport there.
4. Virginia is one of our oldest states.
   The state is the birthplace of several presidents.
5. Many trained porpoises can walk on their tails.
   They can fetch balls.
   They also can leap through hoops.
6. Motorists must obey the traffic laws.
   Bicyclists must obey the traffic laws, too.

Part 2 What Are Compound Sentences? pp. 373-376

Objective 1. To understand the definition of the compound sentence

2. To recognize the parts of compound sentences

3. To write compound sentences and to punctuate them correctly

Presenting the Lesson 1. Read and discuss pages 373 and 374. You may wish to review conjunctions as presented in Handbook Section 10, Part 6.

2. It is recommended that Exercise A on page 374 be done as a class activity. Assign and discuss Exercise B on pages 374 and 375.

3. Read and discuss Punctuating Compound Sentences on page 375. Although a mature writer's use of the comma often depends on personal preference, students at this stage should be held to the basic rules presented here.

4. Assign and discuss Exercises A, B, and C on pages 375 and 376.

Extending the Lesson Have the students rewrite the following sentences, combining each pair with "and," "but," or "or." Ask them to choose the conjunction they think is best to make a good compound sentence. Remind them to use commas where they are needed.

1. Randy would have waited for us. He would have left a message.
2. Suddenly there was a power failure. The lights in our house went out.
3. I love all kinds of pie. They have too many calories.
4. Campers must keep food in tightly covered containers. Bears will eat it.
5. Some swimmers had life jackets. Most did not.

Review p. 377

You may use the review on page 377 either for a checkup or for additional practice.

Using Complex Sentences

Pages 378-388

Objectives

1. To understand the definition of the clause
2. To differentiate between main and subordinate clauses
3. To understand the definition of the complex sentence
4. To distinguish between phrases and subordinate clauses
5. To become familiar with words often used to introduce subordinate clauses
6. To recognize subordinate clauses as sentence fragments, and to correct them
7. To review simple, compound, and complex sentences

Preparing the Students

Remind the students that Handbook Sections 1 and 2 discussed the *simple* sentence, with only one main idea, and that Section 13 taught them about the *compound* sentence, with two or more main ideas joined together. Read page 378, which introduces the third type of sentence, the *complex*. Point out that effective communication, written and spoken, uses all three types of sentences for smoothness and variety, and they have probably been using all three without being aware of it.

Part 1 What Are Complex Sentences? pp. 379-381

Objectives 1. To understand the definition of the clause
2. To differentiate between main and subordinate clauses
3. To understand the definition of the complex sentence

Presenting the Lesson 1. Read and discuss pages 379 to 381, with particular emphasis on the definition of subordinate clauses. When discussing the examples of subordinate clauses, make it clear that these clauses are giving information, not asking. The clause beginning with *who* is not a question.

2. Before the students work the Exercise on page 381, they should realize that every main clause in this set is a simple declarative sentence. Assign and discuss the Exercise.

Optional Practice Have students identify each of the following clauses as main or subordinate.

1. Where we were standing
2. When school starts in September
3. On Tuesday we'll go swimming
4. If he wins the election
5. That we built last summer

Part 2 More About Subordinate Clauses pp. 381-384

Objectives 1. To distinguish between phrases and subordinate clauses

2. To become familiar with words often used to introduce subordinate clauses

Presenting the Lesson 1. Read and discuss pages 381 and 382. Ask students to think of both a phrase and a clause beginning with each of these words: *because, before, since.*

2. It is recommended that you do the Exercise on page 382 with the class. Have students identify the subject and verb in each clause.

3. Read and discuss pages 382 and 383. Have students suggest sentences using the words in the lists.

4. It is suggested that Exercise A on pages 383 and 384 be done as a class activity. Assign and discuss Exercises B and C. For Exercise C, remind the students to consult the lists of words used to begin subordinate clauses.

Extending the Lesson Have the students combine the two simple sentences in each of the following sets into one complex sentence, using a subordinating word.

Example: I found the book. Arlie wanted the book.
I found the book *that* Arlie wanted.
or
Arlie wanted the book *that* I found.

1. The picnic ended early. A thunderstorm began.
2. The family moved away. The family lived next door.

3. Mom will give permission. I'll get a part-time job.
4. The lamp broke. The lamp was an antique.
5. Lucia read a book. She ate lunch.

Part 3 More About Sentence Fragments pp. 384-386

Objective To recognize subordinate clauses as sentence fragments, and to correct them

Presenting the Lesson 1. Read and discuss pages 384 and 385. Ask students for other completions of the sample fragments.

2. Assign and discuss Exercises A and B on pages 385 and 386.

Optional Practice Present the following lists of clauses to the students. Have them match each main clause with as many subordinate clauses as possible to form possible complex sentences.

Main Clauses	Subordinate Clauses
I didn't have breakfast	although the weather was awful.
The farmer worked quickly	because we were out of milk.
Jeff walked to the store	until Dad fixed it.
Arlene's bike squeaked	whenever he felt restless.

Part 4 A Review of Sentences pp. 386-387

Objective To review simple, compound, and complex sentences

Presenting the Lesson 1. Read and discuss pages 386 and 387. Ask the students to explain the differences as the example sentences are changed from simple to compound to complex.

2. It is suggested that Exercise A on page 387 be done as a class activity. Assign and discuss Exercise B.

Review p. 388

You may use the review on page 388 either as a checkup or for additional practice.

Diagraming the Sentence

Pages 389-405

Objectives

1. To understand the purpose of diagraming
2. To diagram verbs and their subjects
3. To diagram subjects in unusual order
4. To diagram questions
5. To diagram imperative sentences
6. To diagram sentences with *There*
7. To diagram compound subjects and verbs
8. To diagram sentences with direct objects
9. To diagram sentences with predicate nouns
10. To diagram sentences with predicate adjectives
11. To diagram sentences with adjectives
12. To diagram sentences with possessive nouns
13. To diagram sentences with adverbs
14. To diagram sentences with prepositional phrases
15. To diagram compound sentences

Preparing the Students

Ask the students if they have ever put together (or observed someone else put together) something like a model airplane, or a bicycle, which came with a diagram of all the parts showing how the finished product is built. The diagram indicated how the parts of the object fitted together to make the whole.

Explain that this chapter will show how they can make diagrams of sentences, and that these diagrams are simply pictures illustrating how the parts of the sentence are put together to build the finished product.

Part 1 What Is Diagraming? pp. 389-390

Objective To understand the purpose of diagraming.

Presenting the Lesson Read and discuss the material on pages 389 and 390. Ask the students to compare any other sorts of diagrams and patterns they can think of.

Part 2 Diagraming Verbs and Their Subjects p. 390

Objective To diagram verbs and their subjects

Presenting the Lesson 1. Read and discuss page 390.

2. Do with the class a few items from the Exercise on page 390. Assign and discuss the rest of the Exercise.

Optional Practice Have the students diagram the verb and its subject in each sentence of Exercise A and B of Handbook Section 1, Part 5 (pp. 221-222).

Part 3 Diagraming Subjects in Unusual Order p. 391

Objective To diagram subjects in unusual order

Presenting the Lesson 1. Read and discuss page 391. Mention that in this kind of sentence an adverb or a prepositional phrase often begins the sentence, and that it may be helpful to turn the sentence around mentally to subject-verb order.

2. Do together some of the Exercise on page 391, until the students show understanding. Assign and discuss the rest of the Exercise.

Extending the Lesson Have the students diagram the subjects and verbs of these sentences:

All around us an eerie wind blew.
Into the stadium blew a gusty wind.
The wind blew my hat into the river.

They should see that the subject and verb are not changed despite the changes in the rest of the sentence, and in the word order.

Part 4 Diagraming Questions p. 392

Objective To diagram questions

Presenting the Lesson 1. Read and discuss page 392.
2. Assign and discuss the Exercise on page 392.

Optional Practice Have the students diagram the subjects and verbs of the questions in Exercises A and B of Handbook Section 1, Part 7 (pp. 224-225).

Part 5 Diagraming Imperative Sentences p. 393

Objective To diagram imperative sentences

Presenting the Lesson 1. Read and discuss page 393. If necessary, review Handbook Section 1, Part 8.
2. Assign and discuss the Exercise on page 393.

Optional Practice Have the students diagram the subjects and verbs of the sentences in Exercises A and B of Handbook Section 1, Part 8 (pp. 226-227).

Part 6 Diagraming Sentences with *There* p. 394

Objective To diagram sentences with *There*

Presenting the Lesson 1. Read and discuss page 394. Mention that, as a general rule, *there* is an extra word when it appears as the first or second word of a sentence. However, it is an adverb when it answers the question *where,* as in *John sat there.*
2. Assign and discuss the Exercise on page 394.

Optional Practice Have the students diagram the subjects and verbs of the sentences of Exercises A and B in Handbook Section 1, Part 6 (p. 222-224).

Part 7 Diagraming Compound Subjects and Verbs p. 395

Objective To diagram compound subjects and verbs

Presenting the Lesson 1. Read and discuss page 395. It may be necessary to review Handbook Section 1, Parts 9 and 10.

2. Assign and discuss the Exercise on page 395.

Optional Practice Have students diagram the compound subjects and verbs in Handbook Section 1, Part 9, Exercise A (p. 228), and Part 10, Exercise A (p. 230).

Part 8 Diagraming Sentences Containing Direct Objects

pp. 396-397

Objective To diagram sentences with direct objects

Presenting the Lesson 1. Read and discuss page 396. It may be necessary to review Handbook Section 4, Part 3.

2. Assign and discuss the Exercise on pages 396 and 397.

Optional Practice Have the students diagram the subjects, verbs, and direct objects in the sentences of Exercises A and B,Find direct objects (pp. 259-260), in Handbook Section 4, Part 3.

Part 9 Diagraming Sentences Containing Predicate Nouns

pp. 397-398

Objective To diagram sentences with predicate nouns

Presenting the Lesson 1. Read and discuss page 397. It may be necessary to review Handbook Section 4, Part 4, concerning linking verbs.

2. Assign and discuss the Exercise on page 398.

Part 10 Diagraming Sentences Containing Predicate Adjectives

pp. 398-399

Objective To diagram sentences with predicate adjectives

Presenting the Lesson 1. Read and discuss pages 398 and 399. If necessary, refer to Handbook Section 4, Part 4.

2. Assign and discuss the Exercise on page 399.

Optional Practice Have the students diagram the subjects, verbs, and predicate words of the sentences in either set of Exercises in Handbook Section 4, Part 4 (pp. 260-264).

Part 11 Diagraming Sentences Containing Adjectives

pp. 399-400

Objective To diagram sentences with adjectives

Presenting the Lesson 1. Read and discuss pages 399 and 400. If necessary, review Handbook Section 8, Parts 1 and 2, concerning adjectives.

2. Assign and discuss the Exercise on page 400.

Optional Practice Have the students follow the directions for the Part 11 Exercise, using the sentences of Exercise A (p. 316) in Handbook Section 8, Part 1.

Part 12 Diagraming Sentences Containing Possessive Nouns

pp. 400-401

Objective To diagram sentences with possessive nouns

Presenting the Lesson 1. Read and discuss page 400. If necessary, review Handbook Section 3, Part 4, concerning how nouns show possession.

2. Assign and discuss the Exercise on page 401.

Part 13 Diagraming Sentences Containing Adverbs

pp. 401-402

Objective To diagram sentences with adverbs

Presenting the Lesson 1. Read and discuss pages 401 and 402. Remind the students that adverbs telling *how, when,* or *where* usually modify the verb. Adverbs that tell *to what extent* may modify adjectives or other adverbs. If necessary, review Handbook Section 9, Part 1.

2. Assign and discuss the Exercise on page 402.

Optional Practice Have the students follow the directions for the Part 13 Exercise, using sentences 1 to 4 and 6 to 10 of Exercise C (pp. 321-322) in Handbook Section 9, Part 1. Point out that *not* and *n't* are considered adverbs.

Part 14 Diagraming Prepositional Phrases pp. 402-403

Objective To diagram sentences with prepositional phrases

Presenting the Lesson 1. Read and discuss pages 402 and 403. If necessary, review Handbook Section 10, Part 4, concerning prepositional phrases as modifiers. Stress that an adjective phrase is placed where an adjective would be placed, immediately under the noun or pronoun it modifies, and that an adverb phrase is placed where a similar adverb would be placed, under the verb.
2. Assign and discuss the Exercise on page 403.

Optional Practice Have the students diagram the subjects, verbs, predicate words, direct objects, and prepositional phrases of Exercises A and B of Handbook Section 10, Part 4 (pp. 347-348).

Part 15 Diagraming Compound Sentences p. 404

Objective To diagram compound sentences

Presenting the Lesson 1. Read and discuss page 404. If necessary, review Handbook Section 13, Part 2, concerning compound sentences. Make sure the students see on the sample diagram exactly where the dotted line begins and ends.

Optional Practice Have the students follow the directions for the Part 15 Exercise, using the sentences of Exercises A and B, Use compound sentences (pp. 374-375), in Handbook Section 13, Part 2.

Review p. 405

You may use the review on page 405 either as a checkup or for additional practice.

Capitalization

Pages 406-418

Objectives

1. To understand and apply the rules for capitalizing proper nouns and adjectives
2. To capitalize first words of sentences, poems, and other writings, where appropriate

Preparing the Students

Students have been familiar with the use of capitalization since they first began to read and write. Two kinds of errors occur frequently in student writing: the use of capitals where not needed, and failure to capitalize words when necessary. The following paragraph contains both kinds of errors.

Write the paragraph on the board or distribute copies of it. Ask students to circle all the mistakes.

> all the trees on Oliver street are Elm Trees. dr. lang, a Biology Teacher at wallis high school, says it's lucky none of them have caught dutch Elm disease. i hope they don't. it would be a shame to lose the cool Summer Shade and the beautiful Fall Colors.

Are students able to find all the errors? (Prepare a similar paragraph for use as review at the conclusion of this chapter.)

Read and discuss page 406.

Proper Nouns and Adjectives

pp. 407-411

Objective To understand and apply the rules for capitalizing proper nouns and adjectives

Presenting the Lesson 1. Read and discuss page 407. Stress the difference between common and proper nouns.

2. Encourage students to supply additional examples for each item discussed.

3. Assign and discuss Exercises A and B on page 408. (The Exercises in this Part are cumulative; for best results, cover the material in the order in which it is presented.)

4. Read and discuss pages 408 and 409.

5. Assign and discuss Exercises A and B on pages 409 and 410.

6. Read and discuss page 410. Be sure that students understand the meanings of the terms *race, religion, nationality,* and *language.*

7. Assign and discuss Exercises A and B on page 411.

Optional Practice Have students write a proper noun for each of the following common nouns, being sure to capitalize correctly.

1. book title
2. soap opera
3. athlete
4. song
5. school
6. river
7. store
8. friend
9. teacher
10. street
11. language
12. holiday
13. newspaper
14. planet
15. movie
16. section of the country
17. ocean
18. business firm
19. building
20. country

First Words

pp. 412-417

Objective To capitalize first words of sentences, poems, and other writings, where appropriate

Presenting the Lesson 1. Read and discuss page 412.

2. Assign Exercises A and B on pages 413 and 414. Have students exchange papers and proofread each other's work. Discuss the answers after corrections have been made.

3. Read and discuss pages 414 and 415. Point out that usually the direct quotation is a sentence within a sentence. Do not dwell on capitalization in outlines unless actual outlining is to be assigned to the class at this time. If outlining is being taught, have the students follow the indentation of the example on page 415.

4. Assign and discuss Exercises A and B on pages 415 and 416.

5. Read pages 416 and 417. Discuss the importance of quotation marks and underlining as well as of capitalization.

6. Assign and discuss Exercises A and B on page 417.

Optional Practice Ask students to bring copies of daily newspapers to class. Divide the class into groups and assign the following tasks. The written lists must be correctly capitalized and underlined or punctuated.

1. Locate and list the titles of five television shows that will appear on the evening of the date of the paper.
2. Locate and list the titles of three television movies that are scheduled for that date.
3. Locate and list the titles of three movies that are playing at local or area theaters.
4. If the paper has a book review section, locate and list the titles of three books discussed there.

Extending the Lesson Ask students to make a collection of examples of capitalized proper nouns and adjectives found in various printed sources, such as magazines, newspapers, direct mail advertising, or church bulletins. They should assemble their findings into a notebook. Make a bulletin board or display of the student work.

Review

p. 418

You may use the review on page 418 either as a checkup or for additional practice.

HANDBOOK SECTION 17

Punctuation

Pages 419-443

Objectives

1. To use end mark punctuation correctly
2. To use the comma correctly
3. To use the apostrophe to form possessives and contractions
4. To use the hyphen for word division and compound numbers
5. To use quotation marks correctly

Preparing the Students

Read and discuss the introduction on page 419. Call attention to the fact that in speaking we raise and lower our voices, or pause, to tell the listener that we are asking a question, showing excitement, or completing a thought. Since no voice clues are present in writing, we must help our readers by using correct punctuation.

End Marks

pp. 420-425

Objective To use end mark punctuation correctly

Presenting the Lesson 1. Read and discuss pages 420 and 422. Ask students to suggest additional examples of abbreviations they know. Have them write their own names with initials. Point out that some abbreviations do not require periods.

2. Assign and discuss Exercises A, B, and C on pages 422 and 423.

3. Read and discuss page 424. Have students write examples of sentences using each kind of end mark.

4. Assign and discuss Exercises A and B on pages 424 and 425.

Optional Practice Ask students to write out their complete names and addresses, using no abbreviations. Then ask them to rewrite them, using as many abbreviations as possible.

Example:	John Allen Whitney	J. A. Whitney
	602 West Arbor Drive	602 W. Arbor Dr.
	Mission Heights, Illinois	Mission Hts., IL

Extending the Lesson Students should learn the two-letter postal abbreviations for all fifty states. Have them create a map bulletin board display that presents them all.

The Comma

pp. 425-432

Objective To use the comma correctly

Presenting the Lesson 1. Read pages 425 and 426. Stress that a series consists of three or more words.

2. It is suggested that Exercise A on page 426 be done orally. Assign and discuss Exercise B on page 427.

3. Read and discuss pages 427 and 428.

4. Assign and discuss Exercises A, B, and C on pages 428 and 429.

5. Read pages 429 to 431. Carefully discuss each use of the comma. Make sure that the students understand when the comma should be placed within quotation marks, and when it comes before.

6. Assign Exercises A and B on pages 431 and 432. Ask students to exchange papers for proofreading. Correct errors.

Optional Practice Have students place commas in the following sentences as needed.

1. Yes I'd love to come to your birthday party.
2. The explosion occured on Friday June 23 1969.
3. We moved from Grand Rapids Michigan to Cranford New Jersey.
4. He asked "Where's the nearest gas station?"
5. After you move the TV set the rocker there.

Extending the Lesson Have students write a letter to the editor of your local or school newspaper expressing an opinion on a current issue. Remind them to pay particular attention to the use of end marks and commas.

The Apostrophe

pp. 432-435

Objective To use the apostrophe to form possessives and contractions

Presenting the Lesson 1. Read and discuss pages 432 and 433. Review the use of possessive nouns in Handbook Section 3, Part 4, if necessary.

2. Assign Exercises A and B on page 433. When discussing the answers, ask students to tell whether the original word was singular or plural.

3. Read and discuss The Apostrophe in Contractions, on pages 433 and 434.

4. Assign and discuss Exercises A and B on pages 434 and 435.

Optional Practice 1. Have the students tell whether each of the following words is singular or plural. Ask them to write the possesive form of each word.

warden	Jess	deer
France	mice	friends

2. Have the students write the correct contraction for each of these pairs of words.

she will	do not	you are
they would	he is	I would

The Hyphen

pp. 435-436

Objective To use the hyphen for word division and compound numbers

Presenting the Lesson 1. Read and discuss page 435. It may be helpful to note these guidelines, also:

If a word has a double consonant, you usually divide the word between the consonants.

Proper nouns should never be divided at the end of a line.

2. Assign and discuss Exercises A and B on page 436.

Optional Practice Ask students to decide whether the following words are correctly divided. Have them rewrite those that are incorrectly divided. Students should use a dictionary to check their answer.

let-ter	wr-ite	syll-able
ofte-n	di-vide	

Quotation Marks

pp. 437-442

Objective To use quotation marks correctly

Presenting the Lesson 1. Read and discuss each item concerning direct quotations on pages 437 and 438. Emphasize these points:

a. Only the words actually spoken should be enclosed in quotation marks; words identifying the speaker or describing the situation are not enclosed in quotation marks.

b. Indirect quotations are never punctuated with quotation marks.

Stress also the correct placement of commas and end marks.

2. If necessary, review the use of commas with quotations, on pages 429 and 430.

3. Assign Exercises A and B on pages 433 and 439. Allow students to make corrections during discussion.

4. Read Divided Quotations on page 439. Some students may have difficulty with this lesson, but they should be introduced to the process.

5. Assign Exercises A and B on page 439 and 440. Allow corrections during discussion of the answers.

6. Read and discuss Dialogue on page 440.

7. It may be advisable to do the Exercise on page 441 as a class activity.

8. Read and discuss page 441. Point out that, as a general rule, long works are underlined and short works are written with quotation marks.

9. Assign and discuss Exercises A and B on page 442.

Optional Practice Allow students experiencing difficulties to work in pairs for the Exercises on pages 439 and 440.

Extending the Lesson Collect a class set of single-frame newspaper cartoons that have one character speaking, such as "Dennis the Menace," "Marmaduke," "Family Circus." Distribute them to the students. Ask them to rewrite the line of dialogue, using the proper forms of punctuation as the line would appear in a composition. Appropriate explanatory words can be chosen to match the content of the cartoon.

Review

p. 443

You may use the review on page 443 as a checkup or for additional practice.

Spelling

Pages 444-456

Objectives

1. To develop general habits for good spelling
2. To develop a specific approach to learning the spelling of particular words.
3. To understand and apply common spelling rules
4. To become familiar with the use and spelling of words often confused

Preparing the Students

Students who use a structured, sequential spelling program need not study this chapter in its entirety. The chapter does, however, offer good information for review or reference.

Suggest that students develop the habit of listing new words they learn while doing reading or writing assignments. Every student, even the best speller, has personal spelling demons that he or she needs to conquer.

Read the chapter introduction on page 444. Stress the need for accurate spelling in all written work. Ask if any students have developed individual schemes or reminders for dealing with certain types of spelling problems.

How To Become a Better Speller

p. 445

Objective To develop general habits for good spelling

Presenting the Lesson 1. Read page 445. Discuss each item thoroughly.

2. Careful pronunciation is helpful to correct spelling. Some words in the English language, however, show no logical link between pronunciation and spelling. Discuss these language oddities.

to, get, her—together	Kansas—Arkansas
off, ice—office	fork—work

3. Encourage proofreading of all written work. Students sometimes have difficulty spotting their own errors, but they can do a good job of editing someone else's work. Try exchanges of rough drafts for your next written assignment.

4. At least one dictionary is now available to help students who voice the age-old complaint, "How can I look up how to spell a word when I don't know how to spell it in the first place?" *The Misspeller's Dictionary* (Quadrange/The New York Times Book Co., 1974) contains phonetic spellings and common misspellings, alphabetized, with the correct spellings next to them.

Extending the Lesson 1. Use the following word challenges to point out the importance of careful letter arrangement in words. Ask students to try to define each group of words with two words that are identical except for two letters that are reversed.

Example: a shiny metal (silver) a small wood splinter (sliver)

a. to desire (crave) to slice (carve)
b. peaceful (calm) a hard-shelled sea creature (clam)
c. growing things (farming) putting something around a picture (framing)
d. person who writes his or her own name (signer) person who makes music with his or her voice (singer)
e. to shape (form) a common preposition (from)

2. Try another word challenge. The word that fits the first definition of each group of words below can be changed into the word that fits the second definition by adding only one letter.

Example: to participate (join) place where two bones meet (joint)

a. a fiery planet (sun) submerged (sunk)
b. a number (ten) a canvas-house (tent)
c. feminine pronoun (her) a brave person (hero)
d. distant (far) place to raise livestock (farm)
e. conflict (war) part of a hospital (ward)

How To Master the Spelling of Particular Words

p. 446

Objective To develop a specific approach to learning the spelling of particular words

Presenting the Lesson 1. Read and discuss the five steps listed on page 446.

2. Have the students apply the steps, as a group,with several words they have misspelled in recent work.

Rules for Spelling

pp. 446-450

Objective To understand and apply common spelling rules

Presenting the Lesson 1. These rules should be introduced over several days (or weeks). Each of the five subsections should be used as an independent lesson.

2. Read The Final Silent *e* on page 446. Discuss the two rules and the words listed as exceptions. Be sure that students know the meaning of the words used as examples. Some students may need to review the definitions of *vowel* and *consonant*.

Point out that adding a suffix usually changes a word from one part of speech to another. Have the students decide what part of speech each base word is, and what it changes to with the suffix.

3. Assign and discuss the Exercise on page 447.

4. Read and discuss Words Ending in *y* on page 447. Can students use the example words in sentences?

5. It is suggested that you use the Exercise at the top of page 448 as an oral exercise.

6. Read and discuss the prefix and suffix lesson on page 448. Discuss the meanings of the example words.

7. Assign and discuss the Exercise on page 448 and 449.

8. Read and discuss page 449. Can students think of additional examples for each part of the lesson?

9. Assign and discuss the Exercise on pages 449 and 450.

10. Read and discuss page 450.

11. It is suggested that the Exercise on page 450 be done orally. What errors do the students need to discuss?

Optional Practice 1. Add the suffix to each of these words and spell the new word correctly.

1. shape + ing
2. make + er
3. entire + ly
4. bury + ed
5. real + ly
6. peaceful + ly
7. copy + ing
8. tap + ing

2. Fill in the blanks with *ei* or *ie:*

1. ch_____f
2. fr_____ght
3. n_____ce
4. _____ght
5. pr_____st
6. y_____ld
7. dec_____t
8. bel_____ve

Extending the Lesson Have students proofread the following paragraph for spelling errors. It contains ten in all. (The errors have been italicized for the convenience of the teacher.)

> It is great to have *hobbys.* Some people enjoy *fling* model airplanes. Others *recieve* pleasure from *hikeing* in the *feilds*. My sister is a *trainner* of dogs, but I am *happyest* when *diging* in my garden. Whatever your hobby is, I hope you *sucede* in *haveing* lots of fun.

Words Often Confused

pp. 451-455

Objective To become familiar with the use and spelling of words often confused

Presenting the Lesson 1. Read the opening paragraphs of page 451. Discuss the meaning of the word *homonym.* Encourage students to learn the spelling and pronunciation of *homonym*, as well as its meaning.

2. Read through the sets of homonyms and other words on pages 451 and 454. Take time to discuss the meaning and use of each word.

3. Have students write original sentences for the sets of homonyms. Discuss the sentences in class.

4. Assign and discuss Exercises A and B on pages 454 and 455. Avoid confusion in checking by spelling each correct choice from the parentheses.

Optional Practice Try this variation on the old-fashioned spelling bee. Divide the class into two teams. One team is asked to spell a word, with each team member in order supplying a single letter. If the team spells the word incorrectly, the other team gets a turn with the same word. The first team to spell it correctly gets a point. Playing the game this way encourages good concentration and listening skills, as well as spelling skill.

Extending the Lesson The two blanks in each sentence can be filled in with a pair of homonyms.

1. ________time for the puppy to have ________dinner.
2. They signed a________of paper promising ________in the land.
3. Our school________taught a lesson about the ________of gravity.
4. ________is the place to________good music.
5. I don't care________the________is rainy or sunny.

Can students think up more sentences for pairs of homonyms?

Review

p. 456

You may use the review on page 456 either as a checkup or for additional practice.

KEYS TO EXERCISES FOR

Basic Skills in English

BOOK 2

WRITING SECTION 1

Words: Developing Your Vocabulary

(Definitions and word derivations for exercises in this section are based on *Webster's New World Dictionary of the American Language*, Student Edition.)

Page 3, Try Your Skill

1. *boy* — borrowed from Middle English
2. *slim* — borrowed from Dutch
3. *snowplow* — a compound word made from the words *snow* and *plow*
4. *UNICEF* — an acronym for United Nations International Children's Emergency Fund
5. *sizzle* — an echoic word
6. *patio* — borrowed from Spanish

Page 3, Now Write

1. *Saturday* — borrowed from Old English
2. *antenna* — borrowed from Latin
3. *boss* — borrowed from Dutch
4. *liftoff* — a compound word made from the words *lift* and *off*
5. *chortle* — a blend of the words *chuckle* and *snort* (coined by Lewis Carroll in *Through the Looking Glass*)
6. *sonar* — an acronym for sound *na*vigation *r*anging

Page 11, Try Your Skill

1. dashed 2. superior 3. spacious 4. fascinating
5. dejected

Page 12, Check It Out

Base words: turn, adventure, use
The *e* in *adventure* is dropped when *ous* is added.

Page 13, Try Your Skill

1. sleep 5. legal 9. fill
2. profit 6. grace 10. place
3. think 7. perfect 11. survive
4. danger 8. justice 12. school

Page 15, Check It Out

1. *im* — not; *immodest* — not modest in conduct, utterance, etc.; shameless
2. *sub* — below; *submarine* — a ship that can be submerged and navigated under water
3. *non* — not; *nonfiction* — literature made up of works dealing with facts or theory
4. *dis* — apart, away; *disagree* — to fail to agree; differ
5. *ir* — not; *irregular* — not according to rule or to the accepted principle, method, etc.
6. *re* — again; *repay* — to pay back or refund
7. *mis* — wrong; *misunderstand* — to misinterpret
8. *il* — not; *illogical* — contrary to the rules of logic
9. *super* — above; *supermarket* — a large, self-service retail market that sells food
10. *sub* — under; *substation* — a subsidiary station, like a branch of a post office
11. *in* — not; *incomplete* — not complete; lacking some part
12. *pre* — before; *preview* — to see or view beforehand, in advance

Page 15, Try Your Skill

1. below + human
2.
3.
4. not + violent
5.
6. not + proper
7. not + logical
8. before + flight
9.
10. not + marked
11. opposite of + tie
12. not + visible
13.
14. again + fit
15. more than + tanker

Page 17, Check It Out

(Suffixes are in italics.)

price*less* — without price
operat*or* — a person who operates something
mysteri*ous* — full of mystery
truth*ful* — full of truth
carri*er* — one who carries
gentle*ness* — state of being gentle
Engl*ish* — belonging to England
mov*able* — can be moved
sens*ible* — having sense

The spelling of the base words changes for these words: *operator*, *mysterious*, *carrier*, *English*, *movable*, and *sensible*.

Page 17, Try Your Skill

1. youth + full of
2. avoid + can be
3. deaf + the state of being
4. courage + full of
5. train + person who does something
6. Scot + belonging to
7. mine + person who does something
8. pity + full of
9. sound + without
10. convert + can be
11. religion + having
12. size + having this quality
13. bright + state of being
14. waste + full of
15. devil + like

WRITING SECTION 3

Exploring Paragraphs

Page 31, Try Your Skill

Main idea: The trunk of an elephant is strong and useful. Sentences 1, 4, and 6 support this idea.

Main idea: The U.S. has received more immigrants than any other country in history. Sentences 1, 3, and 5 support this idea.

Page 32, Try Your Skill

1. e
2. d
3. b

HANDBOOK SECTION 1

Learning About Sentences

Page 209, Exercise A

1. fragment
2. fragment
3. sentence
4. fragment
5. sentence
6. fragment
7. fragment
8. sentence
9. fragment
10. fragment

Page 209, Exercise B

Number 3 is the complete sentence. Sentence completions will vary.

Page 210, Exercise A

1. imperative
2. interrogative
3. declarative
4. imperative
5. exclamatory
6. interrogative
7. interrogative
8. declarative
9. interrogative
10. imperative

Page 211, Exercise B

1. declarative
2. imperative
3. declarative
4. interrogative
5. interrogative
6. exclamatory
7. declarative
8. imperative
9. interrogative
10. declarative

Page 211, Exercise A

1. Which seats are ours?
2. Remember to bring a sweater tonight.
3. Call Debbie to the phone, please.
4. The leaves floated on the top of the water.
5. Have you ever visited the Everglades?
6. Write your name in the upper right-hand corner.
7. How far can you swim underwater?
8. The Swiss flag is red with a white cross.
9. Oil slicks kill hundreds of birds.
10. What a lot of questions you ask!

Page 212, Exercise B

1. Proceed to gate G-7.

2. What a great time we had at Disney World!
3. Please follow the rules of the game.
4 Now, which tooth is loose?
5. Elvis Presley Boulevard is a street in Memphis.
6. Do twenty push-ups.
7. Laura practices the tuba in the den.
8. Does Michael wear glasses?
9. Whales are guided by tiny pilot fish.
10. What is the Continental Divide?

Page 214, Exercise A

1. Dad locked the keys in the house.
2. Thanksgiving will fall on November 28 this year.
3. The first batter struck out.
4. My socks have shrunk.
5. A robin's nest was in the pear tree.
6. Jay's cat eats beetles.
7. The second-string players watched from the bench.
8. We could not see through the curtains.
9. Lisa took her bathing suit with her.
10. The team can count on Mandy.

Page 214, Exercise B

1. Maria found a gold pocket watch.
2. My little brother swallowed a dime.
3. We bought three pounds of apples.
4. My sister's Chevy uses unleaded gas.
5. The sunlight sparkled on the water.
6. Terry's cookies taste best.
7. The final whistle blew.
8. A butterfly struggled in the spider's web.
9. The inventor experimented with the wooden gears.
10. The air conditioner in the office needs a new filter.

Page 214, Exercise C

Sentences will vary.

Page 215, Exercise D

Sentences will vary.

Page 216, Exercise A

1. believed
2. does
3. is
4. boil
5. lasts
6. told
7. writes
8. was
9. guided
10. runs

Page 216, Exercise B

1. ruled	4. arrived	7. is	9. found
2. freezes	5. rode	8. met	10. caused
3. went	6. eats		

Page 218, Exercise A

	Helping Verb	Main Verb
1.	have	seen
2.		stopped
3.	might	beat
4.		is
5.	has	completed
6.	should be	waiting
7.	can	do
8.	had	poisoned
9.		invented
10.	will	begin

Page 219, Exercise B

	Helping Verb	Main Verb
1.	should have	seen
2.	may	burn
3.		was
4.	will	cost
5.	was	named
6.	would	shake
7.		is
8.	has	moved
9.	might	go
10.	must have	taped

Page 220, Exercise A

1.	Helping Verb	Main Verb
1.	has	been
2.	would	take
3.	are	found
4.	are	traded
5.	will	see
6.	had	cut
7.	is	whistling
8.	is	vacuumed
9.	did	understand
10.	may have	finished

Page 220, Exercise B

	Helping Verb	Main Verb
1.	is	looking
2.	are	called
3.	is	mimicking
4.	does	assign
5.	can	walk
6.	must have	called
7.	can	catch
8.	would	have
9.	are	called
10.	was	named

Page 221, Exercise A

	Verb	Subject
1.	coached	Ms. Carroll
2.	has landed	spaceship
3.	struck	clock
4.	buzzed	hornets
5.	did look	cows
6.	is	Joel
7.	were found	treasures
8.	circled	we
9.	could play	boys
10.	shone	eyes

Page 222, Exercise B

	Verb	Subject
1.	worked	Aretha
2.	rises	Dog Star
3.	jams	traffic
4.	cheered	Everyone
5.	was branded	steer
6.	filled	fragrance
7.	can dry	Carl
8.	was loaded	hedge
9.	must have dropped	sister
10.	is	lettuce

Page 223, Exercise A

	Verb	Subject
1.	is	cloud
2.	plunged	diver
3.	closed	girls

4. is	key
5. floated	shapes
6. are	commercials
7. darted	cat
8. understood	Roger
9. scrambled	Patti
10. crept	Kevin

Page 223, Exercise B

Verb	Subject
1. is	idea
2. were	balloons
3. glided	barge
4. backfired	rocket
5. are	creatures
6. is	room
7. won	team
8. thundered	herd
9. is	bracelet
10. is	telephone

Page 225, Exercise A

1. (You) were the winner?
2. (You) took a long time!
3. The (dog) has been fed?
4. The (moon) looks orange!
5. (They) have painted the library?
6. Your (friend) did win the calculator?
7. (We) saw a dark cave!
8. (I) may help you?
9. The (baby) has grown fast!
10. This (snow) won't ever melt!

Page 225, Exercise B

Verb	Subject
1. Does have	hamburger
2. did find	you
3. is	crow
4. Did write	you
5. Have played	Indians
6. look	you
7. Did ride	Angel Cordero
8. had	we
9. Has read	Marcia
10. Am	I

Page 226, Exercise A

	Verb	Subject
1.	play	(You)
2.	forgot	Marianne
3.	Take	(You)
4.	Finish	(You)
5.	Did bring	Joe
6.	Give	(You)
7.	is	road
8.	Is	story
9.	Proceed	(You)
10.	Do know	you

Page 226, Exercise B

	Verb	Subject
1.	Wait	(You)
2.	Does speak	Rosalie
3.	were	players
4.	Did come	explorers
5.	Listen	(You)
6.	Can hear	everyone
7.	do have	insects
8.	Shop	(You)
9.	Turn	(You)
10.	play	Some

Page 228, Exercise A

1. Emily, Charlotte, Ann Bronte | wrote
2. Knicks, Celtics | may win
3. Shirley, Della, Pat | are
4. C3PO, R2D2 | aid
5. Radishes, carrots, potatoes | grow
6. dog, duck | would be
7. John Lennon, Paul McCartney, George Harrison, Ringo Starr | became
8. Marisa, Jorge | tied
9. Cereal, milk, toast | make
10. Mohawks, tribes | joined

Page 229, Exercise B

Sentences will vary.

Page 230, Exercise A

1. I | left, burned

2. Ice | covered, caused
3. family | went, rode, spent
4. Angels | lost, won
5. Frederick Douglass | escaped, became
6. class | rented, visited
7. King Kong | escaped, climbed, battled
8. (You) | Bring, buy
9. Mary Pickford | starred, was called
10. Ed | came, ignored, smashed

Page 230, Exercise B

Sentences will vary.

Page 231, Exercise

1. Phyllis spotted Tom.
2. The dish covered the cake crumbs.
3. The Lions beat the Tigers.
4. My best friend knows Carol.
5. Some plants eat insects.
6. Some nurses are men.
7. The cat heard Donna.
8. That dancer is a boy.

Page 232, Review

	Subject	Verb
1.	newspaper	reported
2.	boiler	exploded
3.	Jessica	should have kept
4.	We	will have
5.	workers	should have stayed
6.	mirror	is
7.	magnet	will attract
8.	boxes	tumbled
9.	helper	is
10.	shoes	are
11.	that	is
12.	(You)	Listen
13.	(You)	Keep
14.	Ramona, Susan	transferred
15.	Cal	lifted, loaded
16.	Are all fables about animals?	Interrogative
17.	Try this new puzzle.	Imperative
18.	The trout is a freshwater fish.	Declarative
19.	What a troublemaker he is!	Exclamatory
20.	Watch this last race.	Imperative

Using Sentences Correctly

Page 235, Exercise A

1. fragment
2. sentence
3. fragment
4. sentence
5. sentence
6. sentence
7. sentence
8. sentence
9. fragment
10. fragment

Page 235, Exercise B

1. fragment
2. sentence
3. sentence
4. fragment
5. sentence
6. fragment
7. fragment
8. sentence
9. sentence
10. sentence

Page 236, Exercise C

Sentence completions will vary.

Page 237, Exercise A

1. run-on
2. complete
3. run-on
4. run-on
5. complete
6. run-on
7. run-on
8. complete
9. complete
10. run-on

Page 237, Exercise B

1. run-on
2. run-on
3. complete
4. run-on
5. complete
6. run-on
7. complete
8. complete
9. run-on
10. run-on

Page 238, Exercise C

1. Gordon replaced a tube in the TV set. Now it works fine.
2. The waterfall splashed down the rocks. It sprayed us.
3. The bricklayer applied mortar. Then she stacked another brick.
4. Chuck read *Freaky Friday.* It's a funny book.
5. Pam dove into the pool. She swam six laps.
6. Annie likes to play Royal Rummy. Evan likes Monopoly.
7. The jury gave its verdict. The man was guilty.
8. Have you ever seen this program? Is it good?
9. In that bakery, a machine kneads the bread dough. The baker makes the cookies.
10. This soil has too much clay. Plants don't grow well here.

Page 239, Review

1. fragment
2. sentence
3. run-on
4. sentence
5. fragment
6. fragment
7. fragment
8. run-on
9. fragment
10. sentence
11. fragment
12. sentence
13. run-on
14. sentence
15. fragment
16. run-on
17. sentence
18. run-on
19. run-on
20. fragment

HANDBOOK SECTION 3

Using Nouns

Page 241, Exercise A

1. Texas, state
2. rules, game
3. heel, boot, nail
4. Mrs. Holmes, promise, class
5. contest, twins
6. lifeguard, platform, beach
7. Detroit, problem, pollution
8. sister, Massachusetts, job
9. porpoises, pool
10. Betty, title, song

Page 241, Exercise B

1. cheese, cracker
2. Alaska, Hawaii, states
3. Pepper, dog, spots
4. foil, sword, button, point
5. prices, coats, tags
6. Sally, Frontierland, streets, houses
7. People, Cuba, Spanish
8. Buttercups, daisies, field
9. baby, smile
10. Mr. Martin, nonsense, excuses

Page 242, Exercise C

Answers will vary.

Page 243, Exercise A

	Common Nouns	Proper Nouns
1.	chair	
2.		Geraldo
3.		Colorado
4.	mountain	
5.		the Rocky Mountains

	Common Nouns	Proper Nouns
6.		Ms. Parsons
7.	school	
8.		Woolworth's
9.		the Hudson River
10.	actor	
11.	country	
12.		Lake Erie
13.		Elizabeth
14.	daughter	
15.	cowboy	
16.		Atlantic Ocean
17.		Green River
18.		Martin Luther King
19.		Elmwood Elementary School
20.	harbor	

Page 244, Exercise B

	Common Nouns	**Proper Nouns**
1.	bridge	
2.		France
3.		Cleveland
4.	man	
5.		the Chicago Black Hawks
6.		Europe
7.		Philadelphia
8.		the White House
9.		the New York Stock Exchange
10.	high school	
11.		World War II
12.	detective	
13.		South America
14.	crossword puzzle	
15.		Coca Cola
16.		Saint Theresa
17.		the Jefferson Memorial
18.	horse	
19.		Monopoly
20.	fort	

Page 244, Exercise C

1. Bob Mackey drove his car to Florida last winter.
2. Ms. Moore told us about islands in the Pacific Ocean.
3. A great many potatoes are grown in the state of Idaho.
4. My uncle once met the comedian Jimmie Walker.
5. Brenda's birthday is in January.

Page 246, Exercise A

1. children — 7, echoes — 3
2. flies — 4, sprays — 1
3. bass — 6, trout — 6
4. countries — 4, adults — 1, witches — 2, elves — 5
5. rushes — 2, bushes — 2, marshes — 2
6. potatoes — 3, tomatoes — 3, tables — 1
7. halves — 5
8. deer — 6, foxes — 2, sheep — 6
9. mice — 7, geese — 7, teeth — 7
10. dairies — 4, cities — 4, losses — 2

Page 247, Exercise B

1. watches
2. guppies
3. wishes
4. feet
5. candies
6. porches
7. leaves
8. heroes
9. lives
10. companies
11. wives
12. women

Page 248, Exercise A

1. runner's
2. manager's
3. girl's
4. mother's
5. astronauts'
6. raccoon's
7. sailors'
8. statue's
9. dog's
10. Tess's

Page 249, Exercise B

1. children's presents
2. Jim's store
3. father's car
4. architect's designs
5. campers' tents
6. Megan's scarf
7. Andrea's painting
8. mice's whiskers
9. governor's mansion
10. Ms. Conway's desk

Page 249, Exercise C

1. king's charger
2. Ma Barrett's pies
3. boys' faces
4. Mr. White's garden
5. Jill's car
6. wrestlers' muscles
7. Anita's earmuffs
8. referee's whistle
9. Barney's cats
10. owl's feathers

Page 250, Exercise

	N	V
1.	Clouds	formed
2.	Jenny	skates every day
3.	The teams	struggled
4.	Strong winds	howled
5.	The dogs	barked loudly
6.	Alex	whistled

Page 251, Review

1. Pélé, soccer, boy, Brazil
2. Rhode Island, state, nation
3. fog, lighthouse, Portland
4. class, Andrew, joke
5. Dr. Alexander, patients, hospital
6. Tracey, seashells, beaches, Sanibel Island
7. Robert Fulton, steamboats
8. People, life, planets, Mars
9. Charlie Chaplin, actor, director, movies
10. Alison, Todd, dunes, Cape Code
11. Papers
12. sandwiches
13. tomatoes, strawberries
14. knives
15. deer, geese
16. sightseers'
17. family's
18. Russ's
19. robot's
20. people's

HANDBOOK SECTION 4

Using Verbs

Page 253, Exercise A

1. held
2. displayed
3. lined
4. played
5. was
6. took
7. reward
8. remembered
9. was
10. missed

Page 254, Exercise B

	Action	State-of-Being		Action	State-of-Being
1.		was	6.	lit	
2.		is	7.	know	
3.	loves		8.		was
4.	rode		9.	swallowed	
5.		was	10.	happened	

Page 254, Exercise C

	Action	State-of-Being		Action	State-of-Being
1.	flew		6.	came	
2.		was	7.	gave	
3.	faced		8.		was
4.		was	9.	aided	
5.	welcomed		10.		is

Page 256, Exercise A

	Helping Verbs	Main Verb		Helping Verbs	Main Verb
1.	was	expecting	6.	had	collapsed
2.	was	hit	7.	has	had
3.	can	find	8.	could have	floated
4.	should have	seen	9.	have	eaten
5.	might	be	10.	had been	hoping

Page 257, Exercise B

	Helping Verbs	Main Verb		Helping Verbs	Main Verb
1.	is	becoming	6.	Did	bring
2.	had	called	7.	Have	written
3.	are	beating	8.	might be	joining
4.	should	eat	9.	will be	performing
5.	can	be	10.	can be	elected

Page 258, Exercise A

Sentences will vary.

Page 259, Exercise B

Sentences will vary.

Page 259, Exercise A

	Verb	Direct Object
1.	found	shipwreck
2.	won	race

3.	steered	craft
4.	am studying	science
5.	have built	snowman
6.	manufactures	coins
7.	will repair	brakes
8.	likes	brownies
9.	eat	turkey
10.	exports	grains

Page 260, Exercise B

1. Corvette
2. telephone
3. game
4. parachute
5. pizzas
6. mainsail
7. assignment
8. meat
9. carton
10. saddle

Page 261, Exercise A

	Subject	Linking Verb	Word Linked to Subject
1.	Jane Fonda	is	actress
2.	hat	looks	ridiculous
3.	bread	smells	delicious
4.	kangaroo	is	joey
5.	bullfights	Do seem	brutal
6.	story	sounds	unbelievable
7.	mask	looks	scary
8.	lines	will appear	wavy
9.	Ebenezer Scrooge	is	character
10.	We	should be	quiet

Page 262, Exercise B

	Subject	Linking Verb	Word Linked to Subject
1.	edge	is	dull
2.	skates	are becoming	rusty
3.	chili	tastes	fierce
4.	animal	is	cheetah
5.	I	do feel	sleepy
6.	trees	are	sequoias
7.	park	is	Yellowstone
8.	Vikings	may have been	pirates
9.	Mother	must be	angry
10.	breed	is	poodle

Page 263, Exercise A

	Action Verb	Direct Object	Linking Verb	Predicate Word
1.	carried	firewood		
2.			is	athlete
3.			seem	short
4.	felt	earth		
5.			feels	cozy
6.	had hit	ball		
7.	made	flag		
8.			may become	law
9.	use	gas		
10.			are	vehicles

Page 263, Exercise B

	Action Verb	Direct Object	Linking Verb	Predicate Word
1.	added	figures		
2.			is	country
3.			has been	guard
4.			seems	sticky
5.	smelled	smoke		
6.	closed	locker		
7.			was	good
8.			became	noisy
9.	stopped	puck		
10.	use	automobiles		

Page 265, Exercise A

1. does, present
2. climbed, past
3. will plan, future
4. saw, past
5. cheered, past
6. is, present
7. will take, future
8. plays, present
9. will return, future
10. explored, past

Page 266, Exercise B

1. will, shall read
2. argued
3. roast
4. made
5. will land
6. wrote
7. picked
8. confuses
9. live
10. will run

Page 266, Exercise C

Sentences will vary.

1. will hurry
2. thought
3. enjoy(s)
4. called
5. removed
6. will finish

Page 267, Exercise A

	N	V	N
1.	Diana	collects	seashells.
2.	Plants	need	sunlight.
3.	My brother	likes	toffee.
4.	Yuri	climbed	that peak.
5.	The judges	awarded	prizes.
6.	Eric	bakes	tasty bread.
7.	NASA	launched	a rocket.
8.	Our team	won	the game.

Page 267, Exercise B

Answers will vary.

Page 268, Exercise A

	N	LV	N
1.	Dee	is	my sister.
2.	Pumpkins	are	vegetables.
3.	This chair	is	an antique.
4.	The Tortugas	are	islands.
5.	Pete	is	an artist.
6.	Mushrooms	are	parasites.
7.	The sun	is	a star.
8.	My aunt	is	a jogger.

Page 268, Exercise B

Answers will vary.

Page 269, Exercise A

	N	LV	Adj
1.	Lottie	seems	cautious.
2.	This ice	is	slippery.
3.	Cherry pie	is	delicious.
4.	Skydivers	are	adventurous.
5.	Jeff	seemed	lucky.
6.	The Cubs	were	victorious.
7.	The sky	looked	gloomy.
8.	My father	will be	late.

Page 269, Exercise B

Answers will vary.

Page 270, Review

1. sets, action, fires
2. elected, action, officers
3. seems, linking, ready
4. borrowed, action, basketball
5. has become, linking, critical
6. feels, linking, fruits
7. are, linking, fruits
8. crossed, action, footbridge
9. practiced, action
10. is, linking, game
11. is used
12. will come
13. must have searched
14. has assigned
15. Have ridden
16. saw, past
17. train, present
18. will name, future
19. explored, past
20. expects, present

HANDBOOK SECTION 5

Using Irregular Verbs

Page 273, Exercise

Helping verbs will vary.

1. printed
2. ask(s)
3. has dreamed
4. wanted
5. have used
6. may have helped
7. confuse(s)
8. listed
9. has covered
10. will like

Page 276, Exercise

1. drank
2. fallen
3. came
4. did
5. done
6. run
7. spoke
8. given
9. gone
10. swum
11. run
12. saw
13. taken
14. drunk
15. written

Page 277, Write It Right

1. come 4. come 7. came 10. come 13. come
2. come 5. came 8. come 11. came 14. came
3. came 6. come 9. came 12. came 15. came

Page 278, Write It Right

1. did 4. done 7. did 10. done 13. did
2. did 5. did 8. done 11. did 14. did
3. done 6. done 9. done 12. done 15. done

Page 279, Write It Right

1. drunk 4. drunk 7. drunk 10. drank 13. drunk
2. drank 5. drank 8. drunk 11. drank 14. drank
3. drunk 6. drank 9. drunk 12. drank 15. drunk

Page 280, Write It Right

1. fallen 4. fallen 7. fallen 10. fallen 13. fallen
2. fallen 5. fell 8. fell 11. fell 14. fell
3. fallen 6. fallen 9. fallen 12. fell 15. fallen

Page 281, Write It Right

1. given 4. given 7. given 10. gave 13. given
2. gave 5. gave 8. gave 11. gave 14. gave
3. given 6. given 9. given 12. given 15. given

Page 282, Write It Right

1. went 4. gone 7. went 10. went 13. gone
2. went 5. gone 8. gone 11. gone 14. went
3. went 6. gone 9. went 12. went 15. gone

Page 283, Write It Right

1. run 4. run 7. ran 10. run 13. run
2. run 5. run 8. ran 11. ran 14. ran
3. ran 6. run 9. run 12. ran 15. run

Page 284, Write It Right

1. saw 4. seen 7. seen 10. seen 13. seen
2. seen 5. seen 8. saw 11. seen 14. saw
3. saw 6. seen 9. saw 12. saw 15. seen

Page 285, Write It Right

1. spoke 4. spoke 7. spoke 10. spoken 13. spoken
2. spoken 5. spoken 8. spoke 11. spoke 14. spoken
3. spoke 6. spoken 9. spoken 12. spoken 15. spoke

Page 286, Write It Right

1. swum	4. swam	7. swam	10. swam	13. swum
2. swam	5. swam	8. swam	11. swam	14. swam
3. swum	6. swum	9. swam	12. swum	15. swum

Page 287, Write It Right

1. took	4. taken	7. took	10. taken	13. took
2. taken	5. took	8. took	11. taken	14. taken
3. took	6. taken	9. taken	12. taken	15. took

Page 288, Write It Right

1. written	4. written	8. wrote	12. written
2. wrote	5. wrote	9. written	13. wrote
3. written	6. wrote	10. written	14. written
wrote	7. written	11. wrote	15. written

Page 289, Review

1. saw	6. seen	11. fallen	16. taken
2. drank	7. done	12. gone	17. took
3. swum	8. gave	13. seen	18. spoken
4. came	9. went	14. ran	19. wrote
5. did	10. given	15. saw	20. seen

HANDBOOK SECTION 6

Using Troublesome Verbs Correctly

Page 291, Exercise

1. Can	3. may	5. May	7. can	9. May
2. Can	4. Can	6. Can	8. May	10. can

Page 292, Exercise

1. let	3. Leave	5. let	7. Leave	9. Let
2. Let	4. let	6. left	8. left	10. let

Page 293, Exercise

1. lie	3. Lay	5. lay	7. lie	9. lain
2. laid	4. lie	6. Lie	8. lay	10. lay

Page 293, Review Exercise A

1. lie 3. may 5. lay 7. leaves 9. leaves
2. Can 4. Let 6. May 8. lay 10. Can

Page 293, Review Exercise B

1. left 3. laid 5. let 7. lay 9. Let
2. May 4. Can 6. may 8. can 10. lain

Page 294, Exercise

1. rose 3. rises 5. raise 7. raise 9. raise
2. Raise 4. risen 6. rises 8. rise 10. raise

Page 295, Exercise

1. sat 3. sat 5. sat 7. set 9. Set
2. set 4. Set 6. sat 8. sit 10. Set

Page 296, Exercise

1. teach 3. learned 5. learned 7. taught 9. taught
2. taught 4. teach 6. teach 8. learn 10. teach

Page 296, Review Exercise A

1. Teach 3. rise 5. learned 7. Teach 9. taught
2. set 4. Sit 6. raise 8. sat 10. raise

Page 297, Review Exercise B

1. rises 3. Set 5. raise 7. rising 9. Raise
2. sit 4. taught 6. Teach 8. sat 10. teach

Page 298, Exercise A

Ruth: any
Jack: any
Ruth: any
Peter: any
Ruth: never
Paul: anything, anybody
Jane: anybody
Paul: ever

Page 298, Exercise B

1. nobody 4. any 7. anywhere 9. no more
2. any 5. anywhere 8. anything 10. any
3. anywhere 6. ever

Page 299, Exercise A

1. aren't
2. were
3. doesn't
4. Were
5. isn't, anything
6. were
7. doesn't, anything
8. Aren't
9. aren't
10. doesn't, ever

Page 300, Exercise B

1. Were, am not
2. Isn't, doesn't
3. Were, were
4. were, weren't, were
5. Doesn't, doesn't, anything
6. doesn't, weren't, haven't, were
7. Don't, any, were
8. haven't, haven't, anywhere
9. Weren't, were
10. were, were

Page 301, Review

1. Can
2. May
3. left
4. let
5. lay
6. laid
7. rose
8. Set
9. sat
10. taught
11. any
12. ever
13. anybody
14. anything
15. anywhere
16. isn't
17. doesn't
18. doesn't
19. were
20. weren't

HANDBOOK SECTION 7

Using Pronouns

Page 304, Exercise A

1. its
2. she, me, her
3. us
4. Your, mine
5. We, them
6. You, them, him
7. He, their
8. I, they, my
9. its
10. We, her

Page 304, Exercise B

1. he, Ted
2. him, Ted
3. it, racer
4. They, parents
5. him, Ted
6. him, Ted
7. He, Ted
8. he, Ted
9. it, race

Page 304, Exercise C

1. it, its
2. he, him, his
3. they, them, their, theirs
4. they, them, their, theirs
5. she, her, hers
6. they, them, their, theirs
7. she, her, hers
8. he, him, his
9. they, them, their, theirs
10. they, them, their, theirs

Page 306, Exercise A

1. We
2. we
3. I
4. They
5. They
6. we
7. I
8. He, we
9. she
10. We

Page 306, Exercise B

1. I
2. we
3. We
4. He, she
5. They
6. We
7. he
8. He, I
9. I
10. they

Page 307, Exercise A

1. he
2. he
3. we
4. he
5. we
6. she
7. I
8. he
9. she
10. they

Page 308, Exercise B

1. we
2. she
3. he
4. she
5. I
6. they
7. he
8. she
9. he
10. he

Page 309, Exercise A

1. me
2. them
3. me
4. him
5. her
6. him
7. me
8. them, us
9. me
10. them

Page 310, Exercise B

1. us
2. him
3. her
4. them
5. me
6. her
7. me
8. me
9. him
10. me

Page 311, Exercise A

1. mine
2. its
3. yours
4. his
5. ours
6. hers
7. theirs
8. his
9. our
10. its

Page 311, Exercise B

1. The rat lost its way in the maze.
2. It's snowing throughout the Northeast.
3. Change the thermostat if it's set too low.
4. That stuffed dog lost a lot of its stuffing.
5. Scoop up that groundball while it's fair.
6. K-Mart ends its sale on school supplies next week.
7. Leave the puzzle in its box.
8. I hate gum when it's stuck on my chair.
9. The school started its basketball season last week.
10. It's too late to go swimming now.

Page 312, Review

1. He	6. I	11. her	16. ours
2. I	7. we	12. him	17. their
3. We	8. she	13. me	18. his
4. They	9. they	14. us	19. its
5. She	10. he	15. her	20. yours

HANDBOOK SECTION 8

Using Adjectives

Page 316, Exercise A

	Adjective	Noun
1.	small	starfish
2.	sticky	gum
3.	artificial	respiration
4.	unearthly	howl
5.	green	darts
6.	Peculiar	noises
7.	white, puffy	clouds
8.	stiff	knees
9.	new	camera
	special	gadgets
10.	brown	wallet

Page 316, Exercise B

	Which Ones	How Many
1.	That	some
2.	this	Many
3.	this	
4.		six
5.	this	
6.	These, that	
7.	this	many
8.	that	several
9.	That	
10.	those	four

Page 317, Exercise A

1. an
2. an
3. a
4. an
5. a
6. an
7. an
8. an
9. an
10. an

Page 318, Exercise B

Sentences will vary.

Page 318, Exercise A

Predicate adjectives will vary. Subjects are listed below.

1. Lemons
2. we
3. boys
4. I
5. sky
6. house
7. You
8. rose
9. Rhonda
10. bell

Page 319, Exercise B

Predicate adjectives will vary. Subjects are listed below.

1. plane
2. settlers
3. suit
4. book
5. loaves
6. plants
7. violin
8. apple
9. leftovers
10. movie

Page 320, Exercise A

1. Irish
2. Austrian
3. Japanese
4. Polish
5. Alaskan
6. Jewish
7. Kentucky
8. Canadian, American
9. Russian
10. French

Page 320, Exercise B

1. Gregorian
2. Siamese, Persian
3. Egyptian
4. Italian, French
5. German
6. Indian
7. Dutch
8. Roman
9. Bantu
10. Italian, Swiss

Page 322, Exercise A

1. that
2. Those
3. this
4. These
5. Those
6. these
7. those
8. those
9. them
10. These

Page 322, Exercise B

1. them, those
2. those
3. them
4. Those
5. them
6. those
7. Those
8. them
9. those
10. Those

Page 325, Exercise A

1. most careful
2. better
3. most
4. best
5. worse
6. latest
7. stronger
8. most
9. worse
10. best

Page 325, Exercise B

1. taller
2. better
3. more expensive
4. stronger
5. smartest
6. funniest
7. heavier
8. colder
9. oldest
10. worst

Page 325, Review

1. These (candles), eerie (glow)
2. Two (batters), new (bats), metal (bats)
3. top (floor), tall (building)
4. Those (cheerleaders), twelve (cheerleaders)
5. This (horse), wild (horse), first (rider)
6. these (apples), juicy (apples), red (apples)
7. Poor (Charlie Brown), any (Valentines)
8. ten (puppies), fuzzy (blanket), blue (blanket)
9. many (pancakes)
10. dry (rattle), poisonous (snake)
11. Australian
12. wrong
13. cloudy
14. filthy
15. comfortable
16. harder
17. higher
18. most complex
19. straighter
20. better

HANDBOOK SECTION 9

Using Adverbs

Page 329, Exercise A

1. how
2. where
3. how
4. how
5. where
6. to what extent
7. when
8. to what extent
9. when
10. when
11. how
12. to what extent
13. when
14. to what extent
15. where
16. when
17. to what extent
18. when
19. how
20. when

Page 329, Exercise B

Sentences will vary.

Page 329, Exercise C

1. there, yesterday
2. Suddenly, up
3. Soon, out
4. hardly
5. outside, quickly, quietly
6. very, carefully
7. never
8. suddenly
9. ever
10. Soon, afterward

Page 331, Exercise A

1. often, more often, most often
2. heavily, more heavily, most heavily
3. soon, sooner, soonest
4. carefully, more carefully, most carefully
5. quickly, more quickly, most quickly
6. well, better, best
7. easily, more easily, most easily
8. slowly, more slowly, most slowly
9. little, less, least
10. hard, harder, hardest

Page 331, Exercise B

1. fastest
2. more carefully
3. more recklessly
4. most easily
5. harder
6. worse
7. more quickly
8. least
9. worse
10. most quickly

Page 333, Exercise A

1. empty (modifies barn), adjective
2. surely (modifies too), adverb
3. really (modifies sure), adverb
4. bad (modifies team), adjective
5. wildly (modifies pitched), adverb
6. bad (modifies boxer), adjective
7. neatly (modifies print), adverb
8. poorly (modifies sang), adverb
9. beautiful (modifies mountains), adjective
10. really (modifies hard), adverb

Page 334, Exercise B

1. really (modifies crooked), adverb
2. badly (modifies was drawn), adverb
3. regularly (modifies go), adverb

4. bad (modifies soup), adjective
5. remarkably (modifies well), adverb
6. slowly (modifies set), adverb
7. incredible (modifies price), adjective
8. evenly (modifies were matched), adverb
9. unevenly (modifies was drawn), adverb
10. promptly (modifies rang), adverb

Page 335, Exercise A

1. Adjective, modifies *look*
2. Adverb, modifies *eat*
3. Adjective, modifies *care*
4. Adverb, modifies *Can see*
5. Adjective, modifies *answer*
6. Adverb, modifies *fit*
7. Adjective, modifies *Kelly*
8. Adjective, modifies *You*
9. Adjective, modifies *reports*
10. Adverb, modifies *do fit*

Page 335, Exercise B

1. Adjective, modifies *route*
2. Adjective, modifies *time*
3. Adverb, modifes *did*
4. Adjective, modifies *pies*
5. Adjective, modifies *idea*
6. Adverb, modifies *speaks*
7. Adjective, modifies *catcher*
8. Adjective, modifies *recipe*
9. Adverb, modifies *plays*
10. Adjective, modifies *tie*

Page 336, Review

1. outside (modifies slept)
2. hurriedly (modifies ate)
3. everywhere (modifies looked)
4. never (modifies collected)
5. today (modifies showed)
6. completely (modifies covered)
7. slowly (modifies works), quite (modifies slowly)
8. far (modifies hiked), too (modifies far)
9. instantly (modifies jumped), up (modifies jumped)
10. always (modifies makes), almost (modifies always)
11. closer
12. higher
13. less
14. most clearly
15. longer
16. steadily
17. plain
18. gracefully
19. truly
20. well

Using Prepositions and Conjunctions

Page 339, Exercise A

1. at home
2. At midnight
3. During practice
4. on TV
5. Without sunlight
6. of scrimmage
7. across town
8. from Stevenson
9. in the hallway
10. into trouble

Page 340, Exercise A

1. over the lake
2. through the dark forest
3. on rivers and streams
4. across the flat land
5. in the third act
6. on a clay court
7. Up the spiral staircase
8. on his show
9. into the dark, icy waters
10. with fudge sauce

Page 340, Exercise B

Answers will vary.

Page 341, Exercise

1. around the *gym*
2. past the *station*
3. to the huge *bonfire*
4. onto the *bleachers*
5. In the science *room*
6. for the lead *role*
7. about the metric *system*
8. through the scenic *park*
9. with a *wrench*
10. Before the final *bell*

Page 343, Exercise A

1. for us
2. near them
3. with Bonnie and me
4. for my sister and me
5. to Keith and her
6. between Andy and him
7. of Britt and me
8. among Tina, Becky and her
9. at Shawn and us
10. behind Danielle and her

Page 343, Exercise B

1. with me
2. toward them
3. Beneath us
4. for him and his brother
5. past JoAnn and me
6. beside Lowell and her
7. to Carlotta and her
8. between Jefferson Junior High and us
9. Between Pete and him
10. with Denise and her

Page 344, Exercise A

1. a. Adverb
   b. Preposition
2. a. Preposition
   b. Adverb
3. a. Adverb
   b. Preposition
4. a. Adverb
   b. Preposition
5. a. Adverb
   b. Preposition
6. a. Preposition
   b. Adverb
7. a. Adverb
   b. Preposition
8. a. Preposition
   b. Adverb
9. a. Preposition
   b. Adverb
10. a. Adverb
    b. Preposition

Page 345, Exercise B

1. a. Adverb
   b. Preposition
2. a. Adverb
   b. Preposition
3. a. Preposition
   b. Adverb
4. a. Preposition
   b. Adverb
5. a. Preposition
   b. Adverb
6. a. Adverb
   b. Preposition
7. a. Preposition
   b. Adverb
8. a. Adverb
   b. Preposition
9. a. Preposition
   b. Adverb
10. a. Preposition
    b. Adverb

Page 346, Exercise A

	Word Modified	Phrase	Kind of Phrase
1.	walked	across the bridge	adverb
2.	rehearsed	in costumes	adverb
3.	locker	by the stairs	adjective
4.	rode	on the tandem bike	adverb
5.	wrote	for her friend	adverb
6.	group	from Sweden	adjective
7.	row	of the theater	adjective
8.	bag	of Cosmic Candy	adjective
9.	jumped	over barrels	adverb
10.	crawled	under the fence	adverb

Page 347, Exercise B

	Word Modified	Phrase	Kind of Phrase
1.	book	of ghost stories	adjective
2.	stopped	at third base	adverb
3.	radioed	to the plane	adverb
4.	life	on Mars	adjective
5.	basked	in the hot sun	adverb
6.	Enter	through the side door	adverb
7.	sped	up the street	adverb
8.	reward	for our dog	adjective
9.	girl	on the bench	adjective
10.	Millions	of people	adjective

Page 348, Exercise A

1. The album by Steve Martin is on that shelf.
2. Annie was praised by the teacher for her work.
3. Blue jeans with straight legs are popular.
4. Buy your tickets for the concert as soon as possible.
5. The handlebars on my bike rusted.
6. The patient with a fever needs a blanket.
7. The book in my locker is yours.
8. The thief was caught by the police after the robbery.
9. The class played a joke on Mr. Pauley.
10. The train from Miami neared the station.

Page 348, Exercise B

1. Kate bought some slippers with tassels for her mom.
2. The pictures on the wall fell.
3. This new album by Billy Joel is good.
4. In the summer, Keith read a book about outer space.
5. The bird with yellow feathers left the cage.
6. My room at home is small but comfortable.
7. The water in the sink won't drain.
8. The car with a flat tire had to pull over.
9. Tom slipped on the ice and sprained his ankle.
10. The poodle with the diamond collar won a prize.

Page 350, Exercise A

1. pitcher and the catcher
2. French or English
3. dries and styles
4. Nancy or Gail
5. breakfast and lunch
6. bacon and eggs
7. clay pots and wooden boxes
8. Running shorts and a T-shirt
9. hit the wall and rolled over
10. soccer or football

Page 350, Exercise B

Sentences will vary.

Page Page 351, Review

1. in line
2. in silent films
3. for meetings
4. of old toys, to a charity
5. to Ken and me
6. Adverb
7. Preposition
8. Preposition
9. Preposition
10. Adverb
11. Adverb
12. Adjective
13. Adjective
14. Adverb
15. Adverb

16. The interviewer and her guest
17. chalk or erasers
18. slipped and fell
19. helmets and shoulder pads
20. roamed the land and swam in the sea

HANDBOOK SECTION 11

Using Parts of Speech

Page 353, Exercise A

1. sky—noun
2. Look—interjection
3. down—preposition
4. walked—verb
5. two—adjective
6. very—adverb
7. upward—adverb
8. and—conjunction
9. me—pronoun
10. wow—interjection

Page 354, Exercise B

1. on—preposition
2. too—adverb
3. Kirsten—noun
4. Duck—interjection
5. These—adjective
6. always—adverb
7. ate—verb
8. and—conjunction
9. into—preposition
10. they—pronoun

Page 355, Exercise A

1. a. noun
   b. adjective
2. a. adverb
   b. preposition
3. a. noun
   b. verb
4. a. adverb
   b. preposition
5. a. adjective
   b. noun
6. a. preposition
   b. adverb
7. a. verb
   b. noun
8. a. verb
   b. noun
9. a. adverb
   b. noun
10. a. adverb
    b. preposition

Page 356, Exercise B

1. a. noun
   b. verb
2. a. adverb
   b. preposition
3. a. verb
   b. noun
4. a. preposition
   b. adverb
5. a. adverb
   b. preposition
6. a. noun
   b. verb
7. a. noun
   b. adjective
8. a. noun
   b. verb
9. a. verb
   b. noun
10. a. verb
    b. adjective

Page 357, Review

1. She—pronoun
2. Oops—interjection
3. smell—noun
4. read—verb
5. rock—adjective
6. Steve—noun
7. Ingrid—noun
8. platypus—noun
9. and—conjunction
10. hungrily—adverb
11. kills—verb
12. Everyone—pronoun
13. or—conjunction
14. Look out—interjection
15. soon—adverb
16. art—noun
17. over—preposition
18. center—noun
19. over—adverb
20. through—preposition

HANDBOOK SECTION 12

Making Subjects and Verbs Agree

Page 360, Exercise A

1. plural
2. singular
3. singular
4. singular
5. plural
6. plural
7. plural
8. singular
9. plural
10. plural

Page 360, Exercise B

1. set, is (singular)
2. Angela, likes (singular)
3. taste, is (singular)
4. We, are using (plural)
5. Woody, plays (singular)
6. students, will audition (plural)
7. I, walked (singular)
8. brakes, need (plural)
9. winds, blew (plural)
10. calls, costs (singular)

Page 361, Exercise A

1. were
2. have
3. are
4. has
5. are
6. Are
7. have
8. is
9. doesn't
10. are

Page 362, Exercise B

1. has
2. are
3. were
4. are
5. are
6. Aren't
7. were
8. Does
9. are
10. are

Page 363, Exercise A

1. swims (in our class)
2. was (of the propellers)
3. is (of you girls)
4. has (of the cats)
5. is (of the faucets)
6. has (of the uniforms)
7. tells (of the digital clocks)
8. was (from both classes)
9. is (of the displays)
10. Has (of you)

Page 364, Exercise B

1. has (of the teams)
2. is (of those games)
3. is (of my keys)
4. yells (in the stands)
5. sells (of the vendors)
6. is (of my toes)
7. Does (in the room)
8. eats (with braces)
9. throws (of the pitchers)
10. weighs (of those elephants)

Page 365, Exercise A

1. does
2. is
3. was
4. were
5. is
6. are
7. is
8. were
9. is
10. do

Page 365, Exercise B

1. is
2. has
3. are
4. are
5. are
6. was
7. are
8. Have
9. do
10. is

Page 366, Exercise A

1. sleep
2. I, like
3. have
4. children, walk
5. boys, have
6. were
7. melon, weighs
8. practice
9. phone, works
10. members, are

Page 366, Exercise B

1. Spiderman, is
2. are
3. share
4. raincoat, keeps
5. waffles, are
6. skateboard, goes
7. have
8. sisters, have
9. watch, is
10. buzzer, signals

Page 367, Exercise A

1. were
2. am
3. are
4. ride
5. am
6. are
7. Have
8. am
9. Were
10. are

Page 368, Exercise B

1. were
2. was
3. Do
4. am
5. know
6. have
7. am
8. Were
9. was
10. were

Page 369, Review

1. blast
2. directs
3. is
4. look
5. make
6. are
7. has
8. do
9. needs
10. stops
11. is
12. does
13. are
14. are
15. are
16. is
17. have
18. see
19. were
20. am

HANDBOOK SECTION 13

Using Compound Sentences

Page 372, Exercise A

1. Nancy, Dennis | took
2. Greg | is practicing
3. class | uses
4. Raiders | Did score
5. troops | arrived
6. West High School | has
7. We | learned, practiced
8. Mom, Julie | painted
9. fingers toes | are
10. cat | clawed, chewed

Page 372, Exercise B

1. restaurant | opened
2. people | need
3. I | like, play
4. store, theater | are closed
5. Fans | filled, cheered
6. Mr. Homer | poured, did
7. Ms. Jackson | writes
8. magician, assistant | rehearsed
9. truck, train | collided
10. Josh | bought, fixed

Page 372, Exercise C

Sentences will vary.

Page 374, Exercise A

	Subject Verb	Conjunction	Subject Verb
1.	We | take	or	we | walk
2.	heart | is	and	it | pumps
3.	traders | go	and	they | look
4.	We | have	but	it | is
5.	Patchwork | is	but	it | is
6.	Seaweed | can be eaten	and	it | is
7.	teacher | called	but	she | had forgotten
8.	(You) | Wear	or	you | will be
9.	Mary | saddled	and	she | helped
10.	Winter Olympics | have started	and	they | are

Page 374, Exercise B

	Subject Verb	Conjunction	Subject Verb
1.	Vic | owes	but	he | is
2.	bottle | washed	and	note | was
3.	Jennifer | felt	and	she | called
4.	Bradley | organized	and	Mr. Chan | coached
5.	(You) | Take	and	you | will feel
6.	(You) | Handle	or	they | will break
7.	library | has	and	I | have read
8.	Peter | is	but	he | did play
9.	Sarah | wanted	but	she | could decide
10.	Clay, Steve | must leave	or	they | will miss

Page 375, Exercise A

1. and
2. , and
3. , and
4. , but
5. , but
6. , and
7. and
8. ,but
9. , or
10. , but

Page 376, Exercise B

1. , but
2. , and
3. and
4. but
5. , and
6. , and
7. ,but
8. ,or
9. , and
10. , or

Page 376, Exercise C

Sentences will vary.

Page 377, Review

1. Lifejackets, are used
2. Boats, docked
3. Governor, Senator, spoke
4. Chris, waited, worried
5. Jane Goodall, went, studied

	Subject Verb	Comma	Subject Verb
6.	Bird I hit	,and	Indiana State I won
7.	We I washed	,and	it I looked
8.	van I pulled	,and	friends I jumped
9.	airport I closed	,and	people I were stranded
10.	(You) I Use	,or	it I may be stolen
11.	you I are going	,or	you I will stay
12.	pool I will open	,and	we I will take
13.	Sue I smiled		Tom I smiled
14.	fire I was	,but	it I was
15.	inches I fell	,and	we I shoveled
16.	Vacation I will begin	,and	everyone I is
17.	light I flashed	,and	car I began
18.	astronaut I talked	,and	we I learned
19.	We I need	,or	we I will reach
20.	thermometer I measures	,and	barometer I measures

HANDBOOK SECTION 14

Using Complex Sentences

Page 381, Exercise

1. subordinate
2. main
3. main
4. subordinate
5. subordinate
6. main
7. subordinate
8. subordinate
9. main
10. subordinate

Page 382, Exercise

1. clause
2. clause
3. phrase
4. clause
5. phrase
6. clause
7. phrase
8. phrase
9. clause
10. clause

Page 383, Exercise A

	Clause	Subject	Verb
1.	Since she was six	she	was
2.	because he was scared	he	was
3.	when the game starts	game	starts
4.	that has triplets	that	has
5.	before the race began	race	began
6.	where we meet	we	meet
7.	As we talked	we	talked
8.	that I liked best	I	liked
9.	who had their own TV show	who	had
10.	while you listen to music	you	listen

Page 384, Exercise B

	Clause	Subject	Verb
1.	who is a teenager	who	is
2.	whenever the doorbell rings	doorbell	rings
3.	how actors are trained	actors	are trained
4.	while Mom and I waited	Mom, I	waited
5.	that he was a time traveler	he	was
6.	After choir practice ended	practice	ended
7.	that I saw	I	saw
8.	Although it looks easy	it	looks
9.	what makes them happy	what	makes
10.	after school is out	school	is

Page 384, Exercise C

Sentences will vary.

Page 385, Exercise A

Sentence completions will vary.

1. sentence
2. fragment
3. fragment
4. fragment
5. sentence
6. fragment
7. fragment
8. sentence
9. sentence
10. fragment

Page 385, Exercise B

Sentence completions will vary.

1. fragment
2. fragment
3. sentence
4. fragment
5. sentence
6. fragment
7. sentence
8. sentence
9. sentence
10. fragment

Page 387, Exercise A

1. simple
2. compound
3. complex
4. simple
5. simple
6. compound
7. complex
8. compound
9. complex
10. complex

Page 387, Exercise B

1. complex
2. complex
3. simple
4. compound
5. simple
6. simple
7. compound
8. complex
9. complex
10. complex

Page 388, Review

1. Although we were tired
2. who comes from Italy
3. that your ears were pierced
4. Before I was six

5. When Dad is angry
6. after the robbers had fled
7. whenever the weather is good
8. who is my oldest brother
9. if you need a ride
10. that was terrifying
11. where the best beaches are
12. that was twelve hundred feet high
13. as the chief explained
14. who called that penalty
15. who reminded us of Tatum O'Neal
16. simple
17. compound
18. complex
19. complex
20. simple

HANDBOOK SECTION 15

Diagraming the Sentence

Page 390, Exercise

1. Mr. Rosen | skis
2. Marcy | sneezed
3. Bulls | charge
4. Darren | laughed
5. Horns | honked
6. Tammy Dillon | left
7. candy | melted
8. floors | creaked
9. Mayor Best | campaigned
10. Falcons | will play

Page 391, Exercise

1. Miller | skated
2. wallet | lay
3. patches | were
4. star | shot
5. cat | rested
6. boat | sank
7. snake | wound
8. swimmers | raced
9. drawer | was
10. foghorn | blared

Page 392, Exercise

1. Natalie Cole | Will sing
2. you | Have noticed
3. paint | Did dry
4. we | Shall sit
5. sherbet | Has melted
6. you | Would like
7. school | will begin
8. you | Did get
9. Jennifer | Has learned
10. you | Did enjoy

Page 393, Exercise

1. (You) | Remember
2. (You) | Consider
3. (You) | Throw
4. (You) | Find
5. (You) | Hold
6. (You) | Close
7. (You) | Change
8. (You) | Watch
9. (You) | Observe
10. (You) | Store

Page 394, Exercise

1. There / notes | are
2. There / hundreds | are
3. There / pounds | are
4. There / milk | is
5. There / package | Was
6. There / room | is
7. there / sand-crabs | Were
8. There / time | is
9. There / horses | are
10. There / cards | Are

Page 395, Exercise

1. 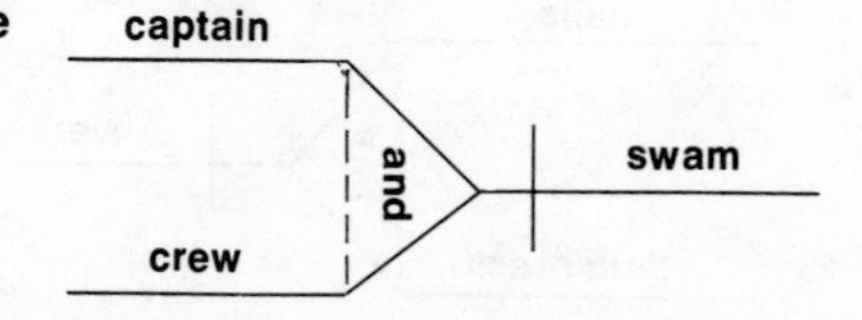

2.

3.

4.

5.

6.

7.

8.

9.

10.

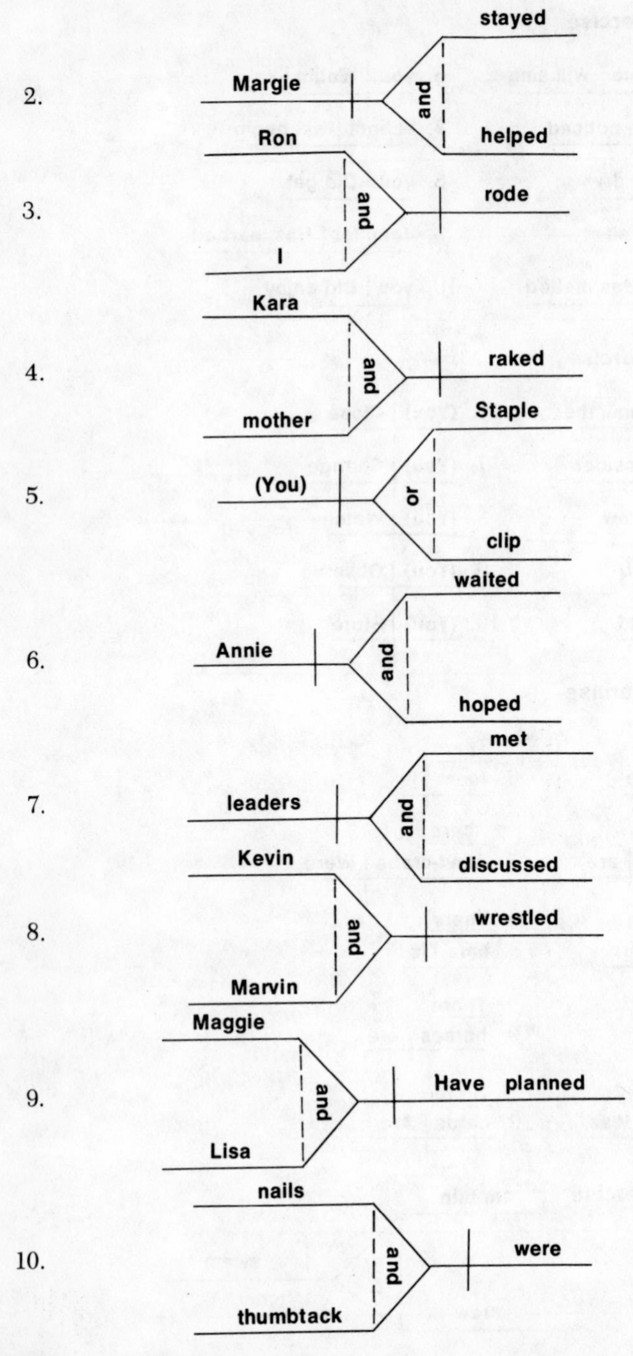
Margie
stayed
and
helped
Ron
and
I
rode
Kara
and
mother
raked
(You)
Staple
or
clip
Annie
waited
and
hoped
leaders
met
and
discussed
Kevin
and
Marvin
wrestled
Maggie
and
Lisa
Have planned
nails
and
thumbtack
were

Page 396, Exercise

1. Dawn | plays | saxophone

2. stars | guide | sailors

3. Noel | makes | jewelry

4. you | Did weave | cloth

5. People | built | castles and statues

6. Jamie | Is using | telephone

7. family | uses | van

8. Dogs | can hear | sounds

9. (You) | Put | name and address

10. Mark | has played | defense and offense

Page 398, Exercise

1. girls | are \ skaters

2. boy | is \ model

3. Canoes | are \ boats

4. Tiant | was \ pitcher

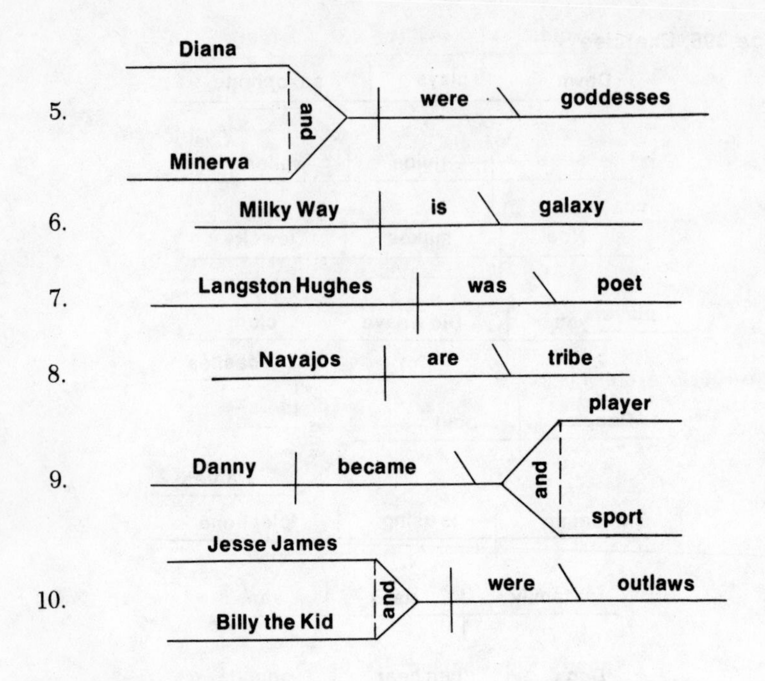

Page 399, Exercise

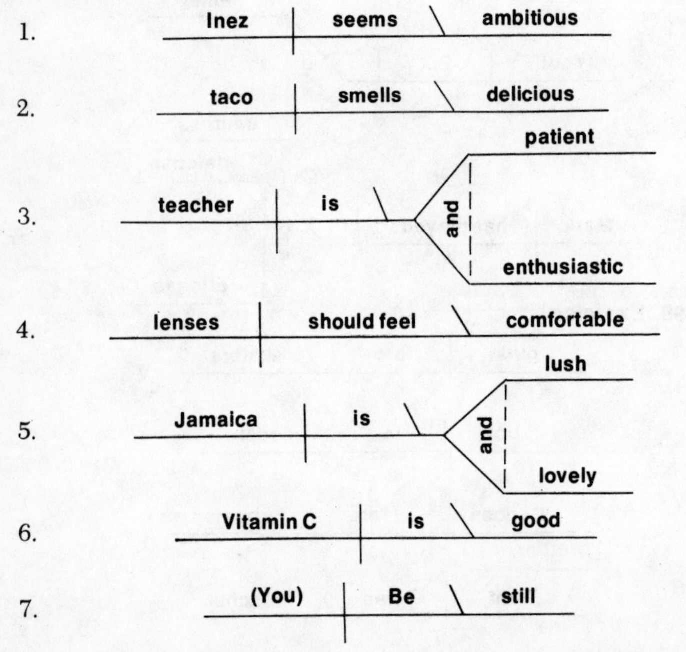

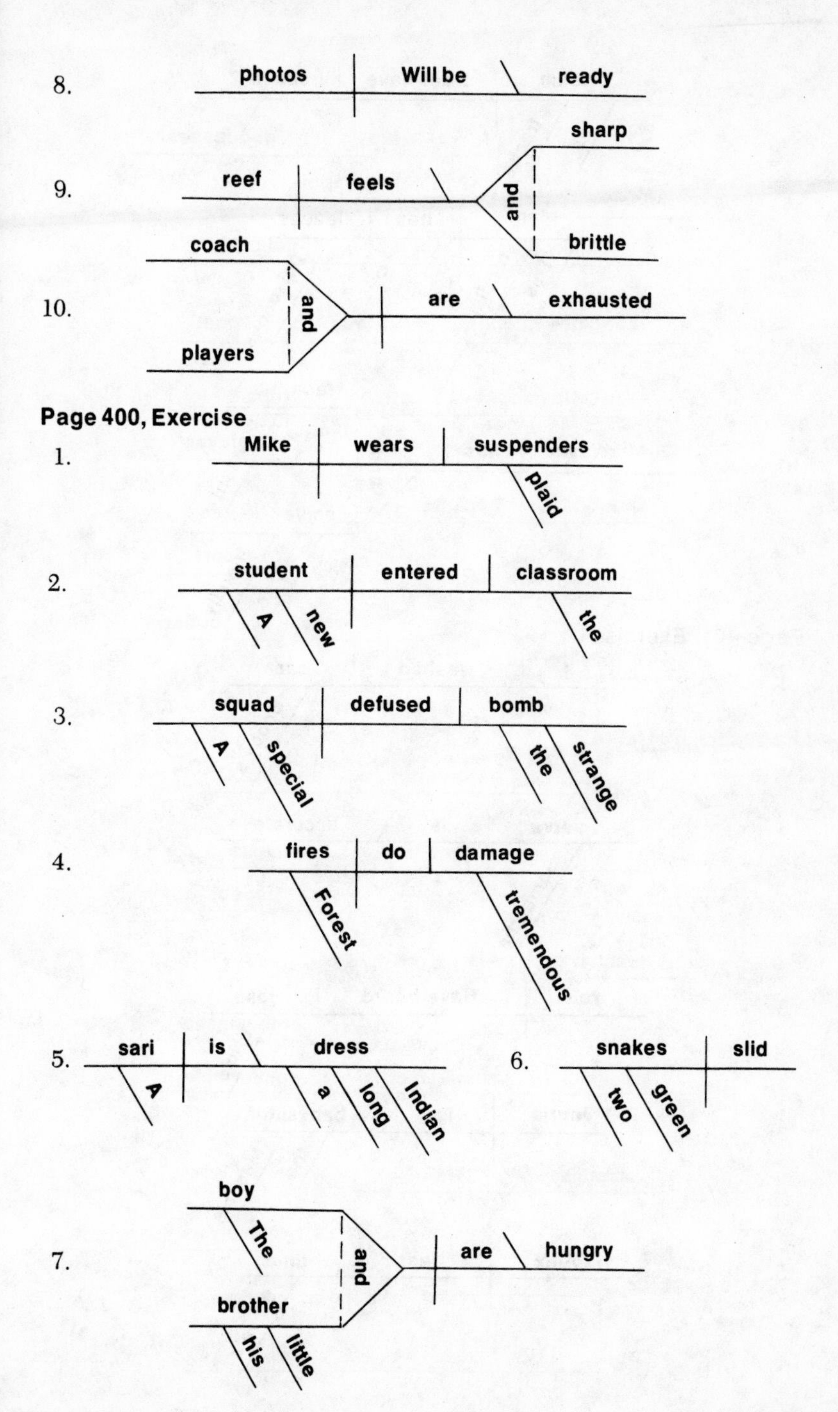
8.
photos
Will be
ready
9.
reef
feels
sharp
and
brittle
10.
coach
and
players
are
exhausted
Page 400, Exercise
1.
Mike
wears
suspenders
plaid
2.
student
A
new
entered
classroom
the
3.
squad
A
special
defused
bomb
the
strange
4.
fires
Forest
do
damage
tremendous
5.
sari
A
is
dress
a
long
Indian
6.
snakes
two
green
slid
7.
boy
The
and
brother
his
little
are
hungry

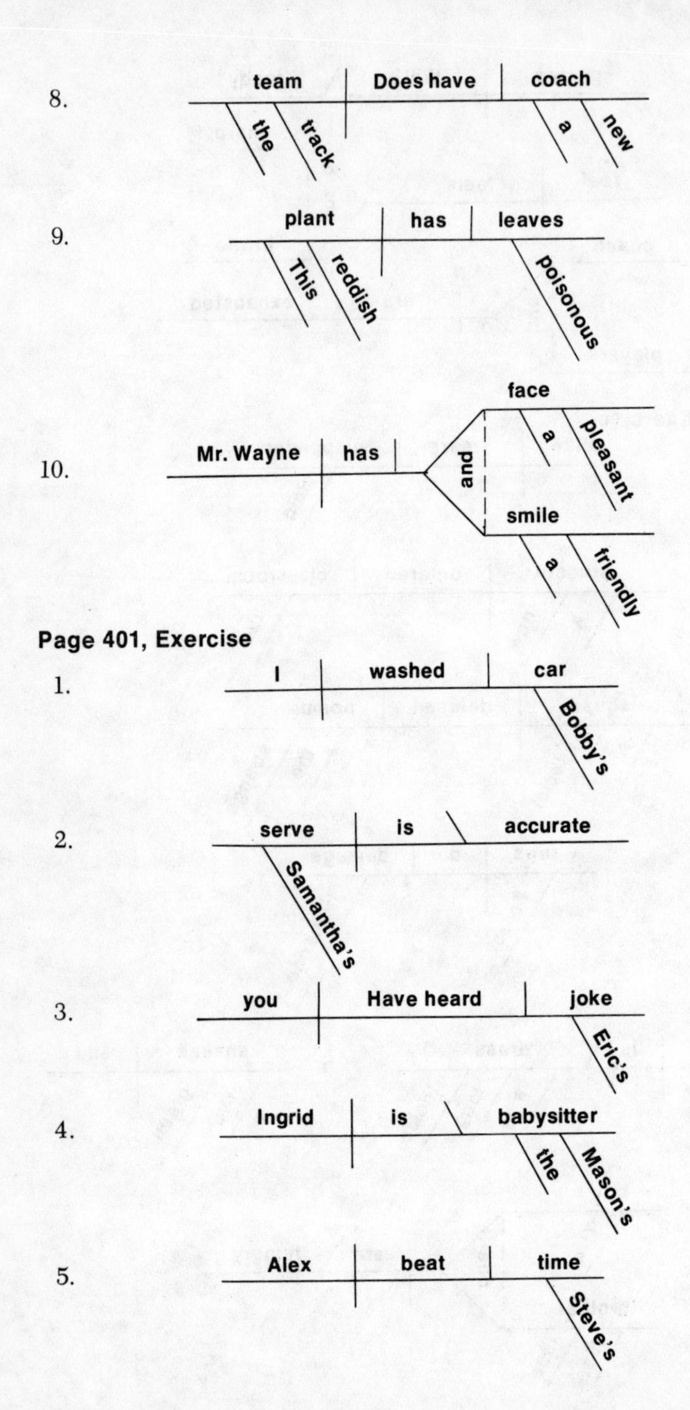
8.
team
Does have
coach
the
track
a
new
9.
plant
has
leaves
This
reddish
poisonous
10.
Mr. Wayne
has
and
face
a
pleasant
smile
a
friendly
Page 401, Exercise
1.
I
washed
car
Bobby's
2.
serve
is
accurate
Samantha's
3.
you
Have heard
joke
Eric's
4.
Ingrid
is
babysitter
the
Mason's
5.
Alex
beat
time
Steve's

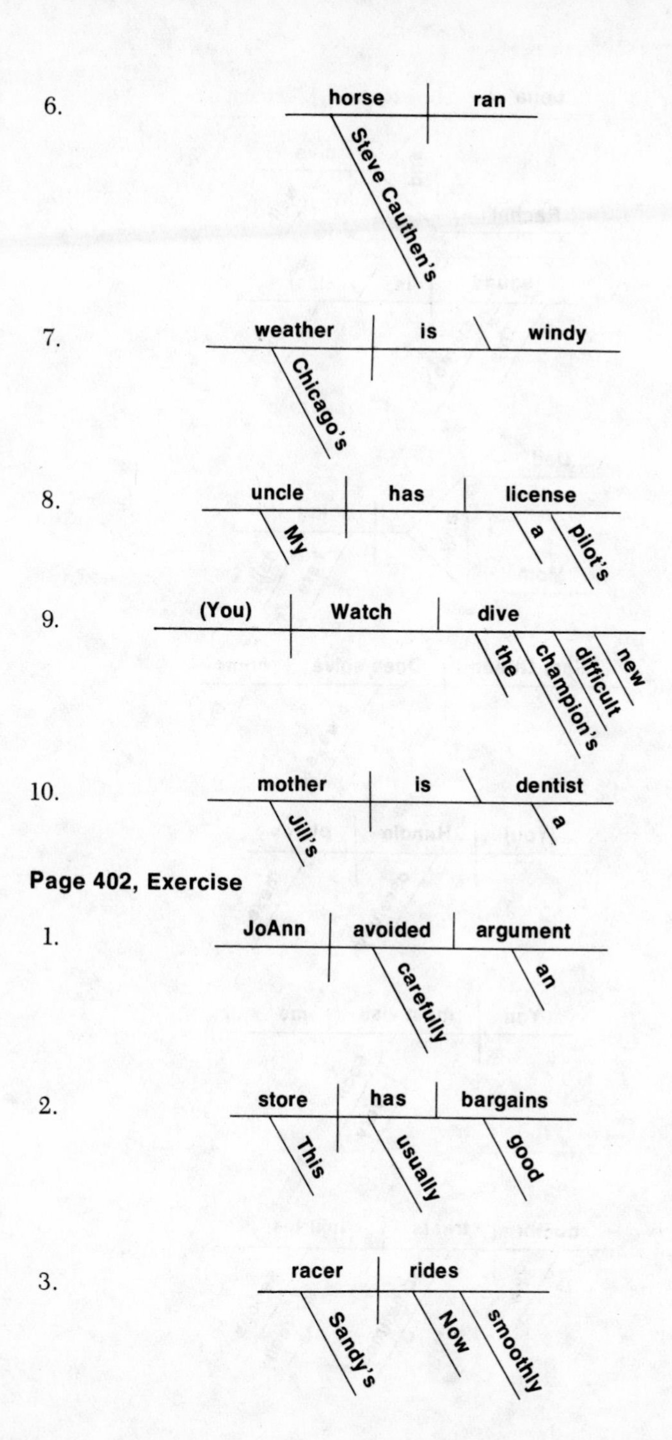

Page 402, Exercise

4.
5.
6.
7.
8.
9.
10.

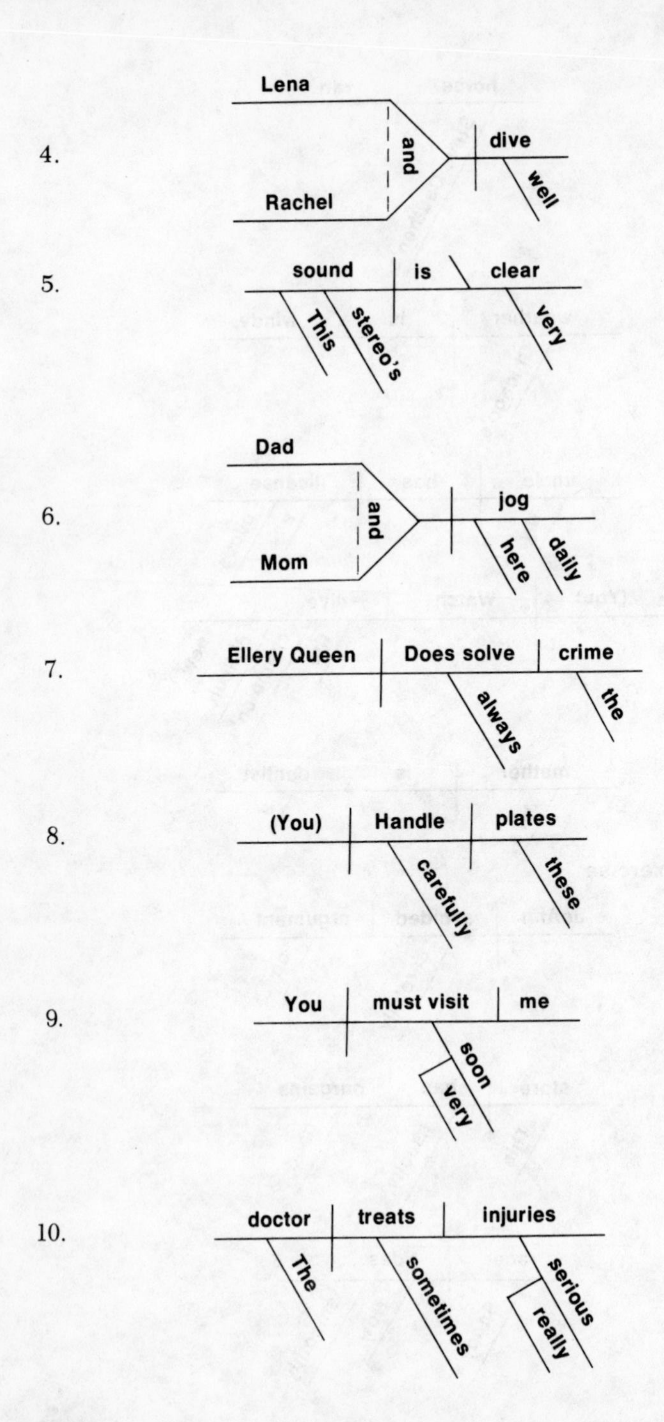

Lena
and
Rachel
dive
well
sound
is
clear
This
stereo's
very
Dad
and
Mom
jog
here
daily
Ellery Queen
Does solve
crime
always
the
(You)
Handle
plates
carefully
these
You
must visit
me
soon
very
doctor
treats
injuries
The
sometimes
serious
really

Page 403, Exercise

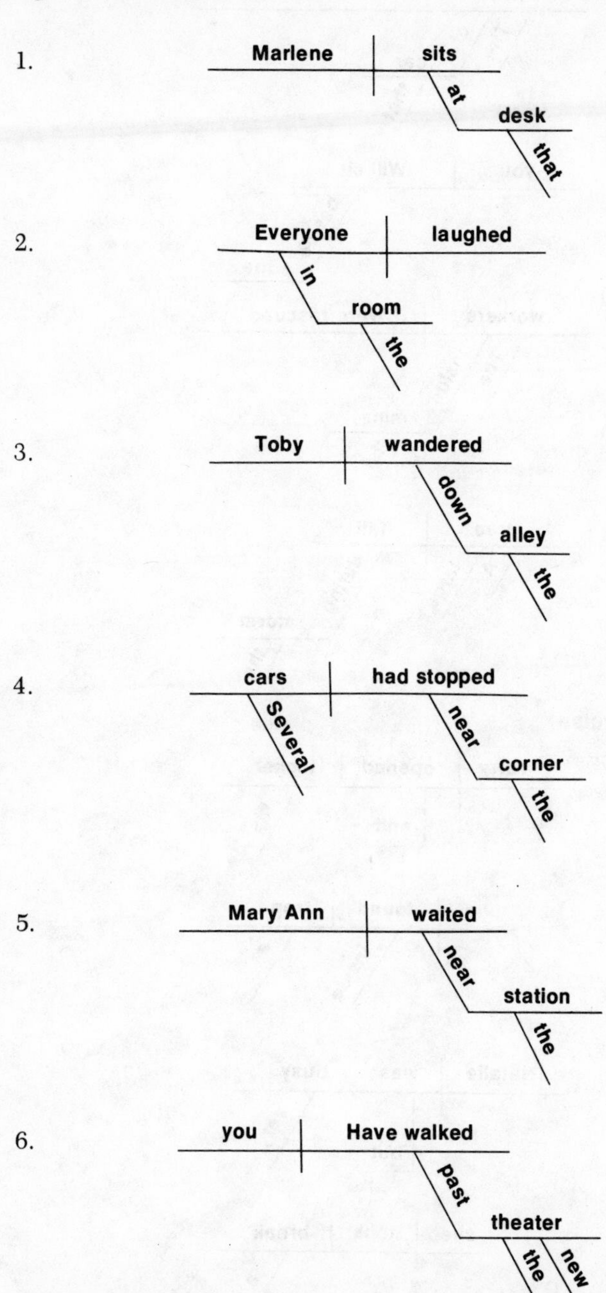

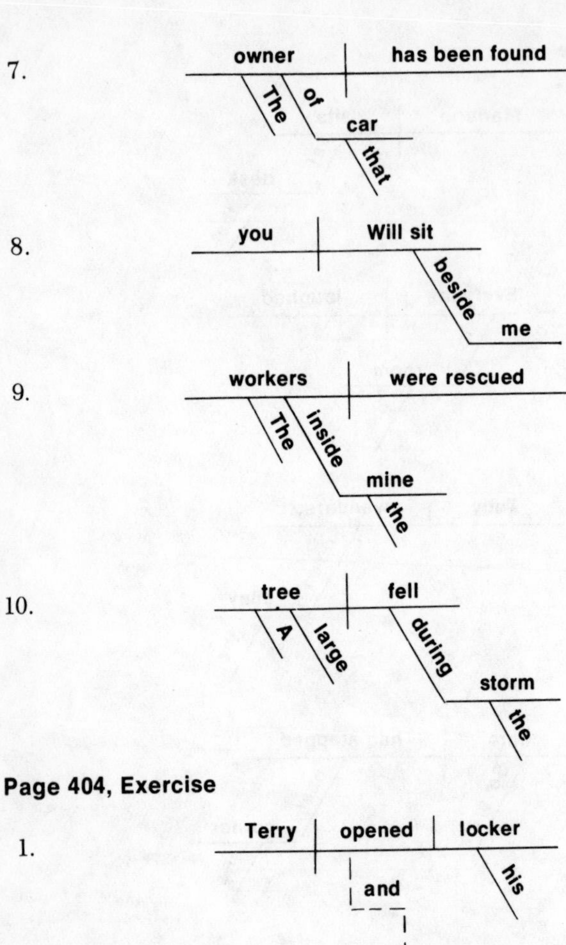

Page 404, Exercise

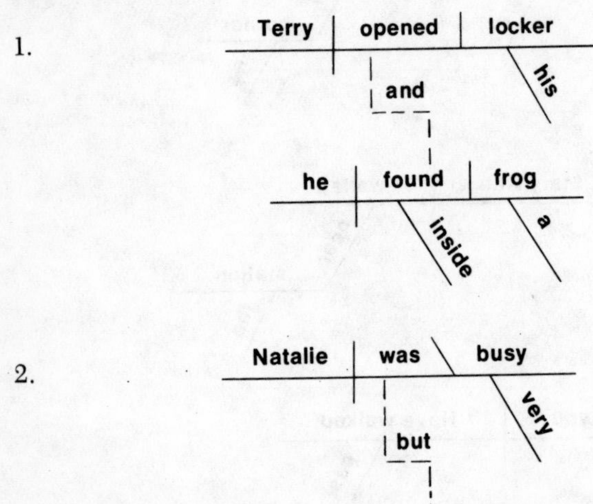

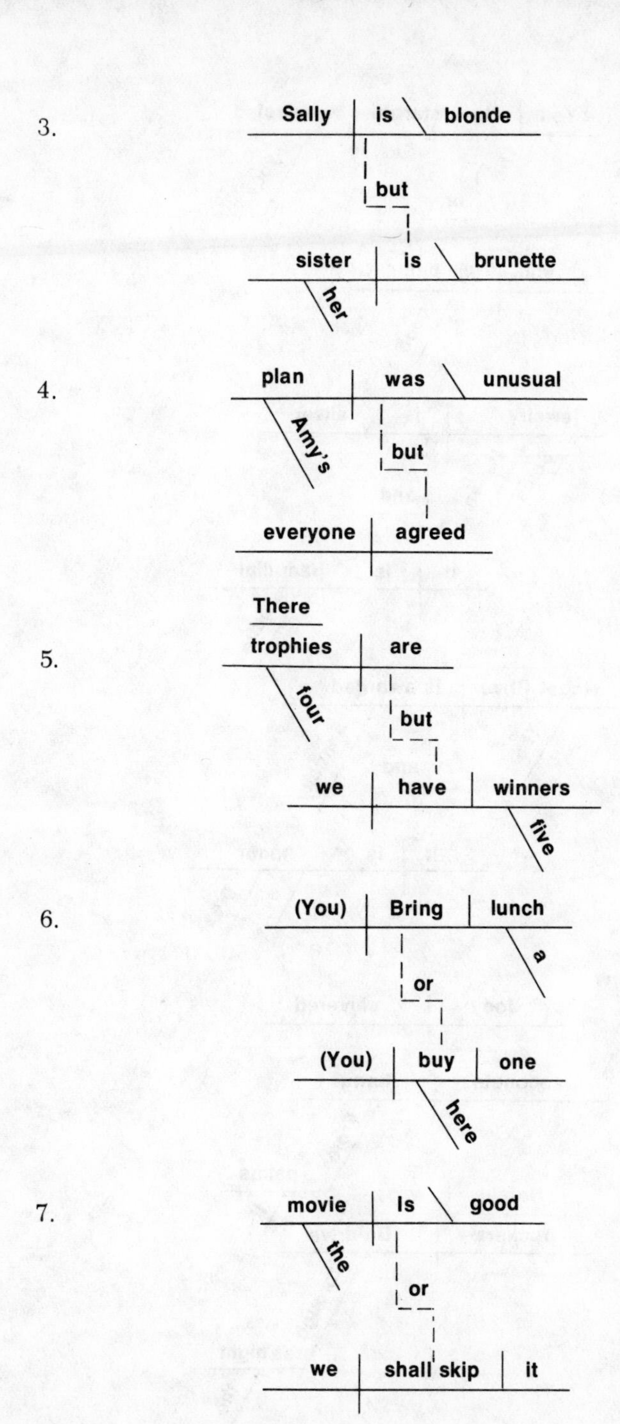
3.
Sally
is
blonde
but
sister
is
brunette
her
4.
plan
was
unusual
Amy's
but
everyone
agreed
There
trophies
are
5.
four
but
we
have
winners
five
6.
(You)
Bring
lunch
a
or
(You)
buy
one
here
7.
movie
Is
good
the
or
we
shall skip
it

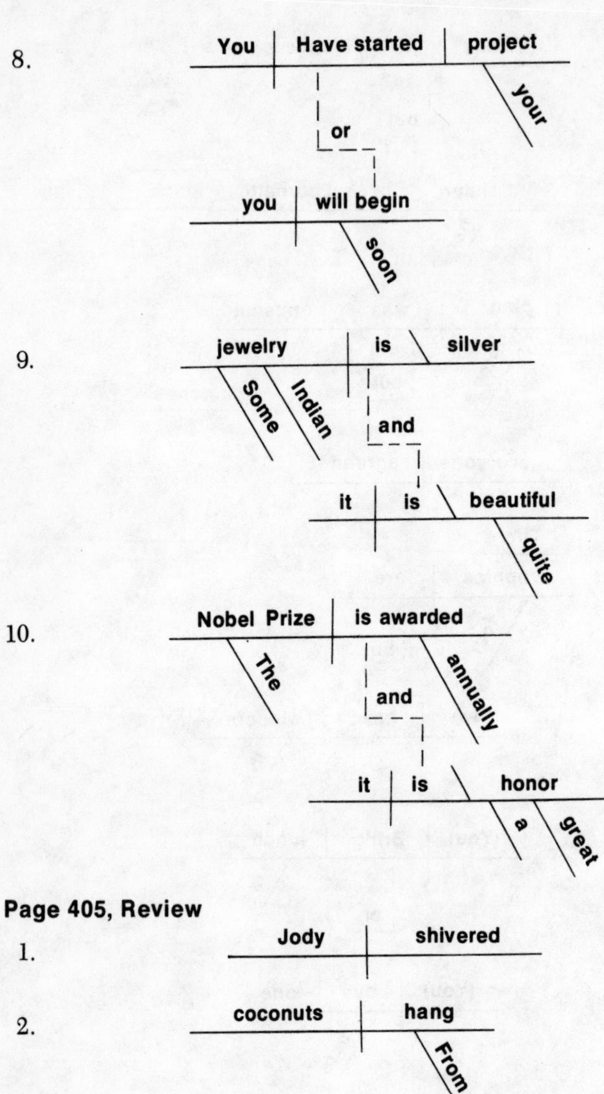

Page 405, Review

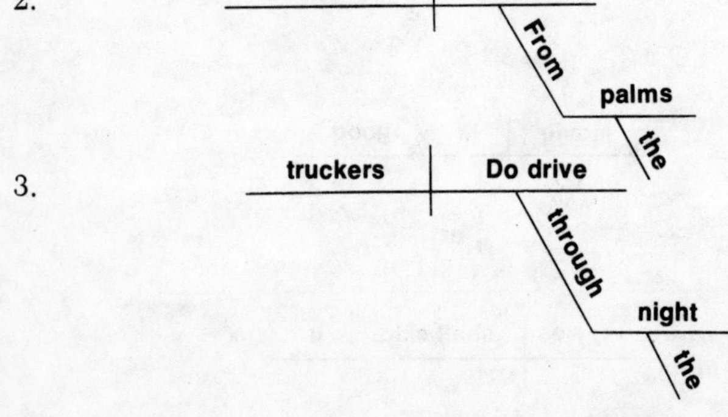

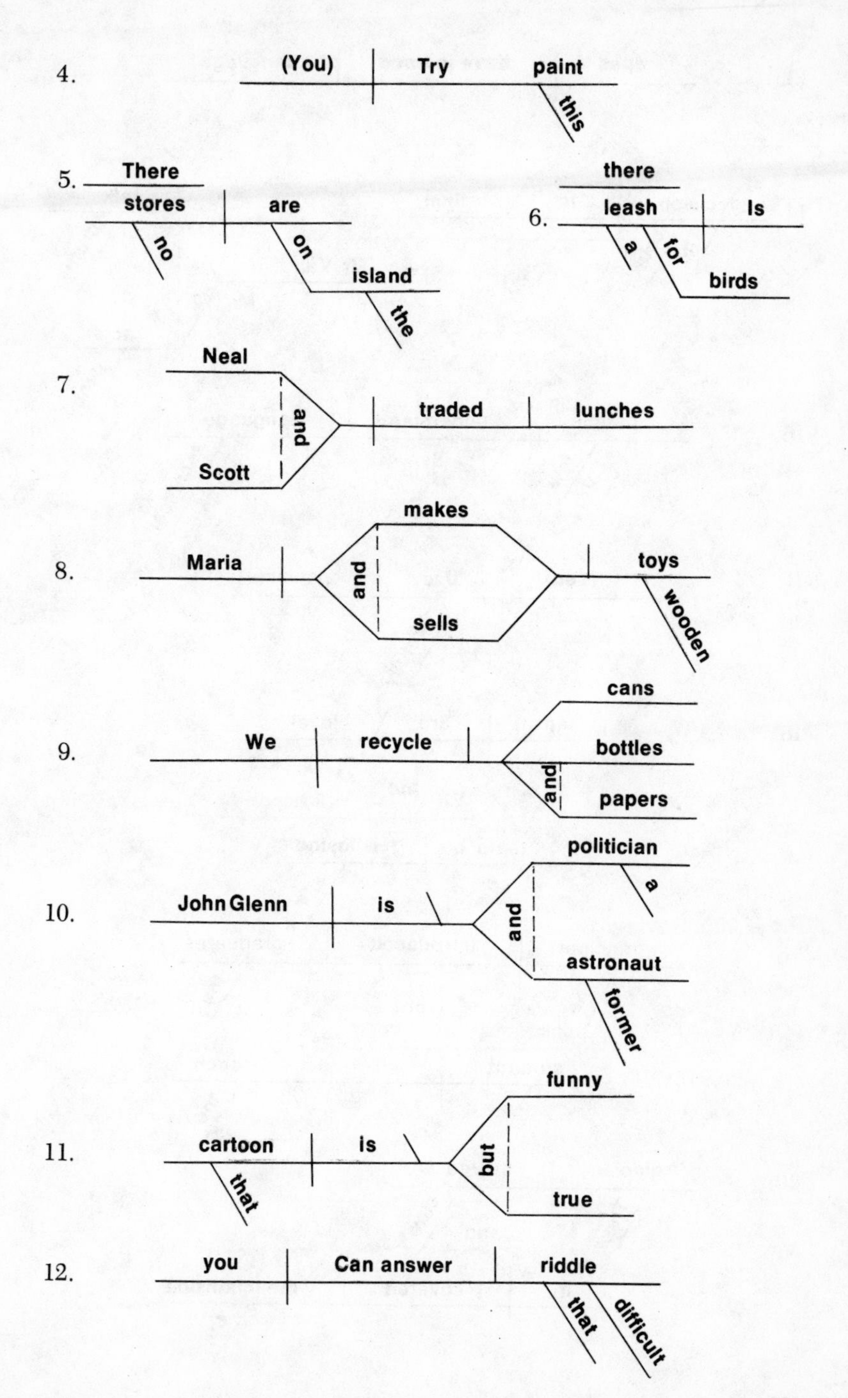
4.
(You)
Try
paint
this
5.
There
stores
are
no
on
island
the
6.
there
leash
Is
a
for
birds
7.
Neal
and
Scott
traded
lunches
8.
Maria
makes
and
sells
toys
wooden
9.
We
recycle
cans
bottles
and
papers
10.
John Glenn
is
politician
a
and
astronaut
former
11.
cartoon
that
is
funny
but
true
12.
you
Can answer
riddle
that
difficult

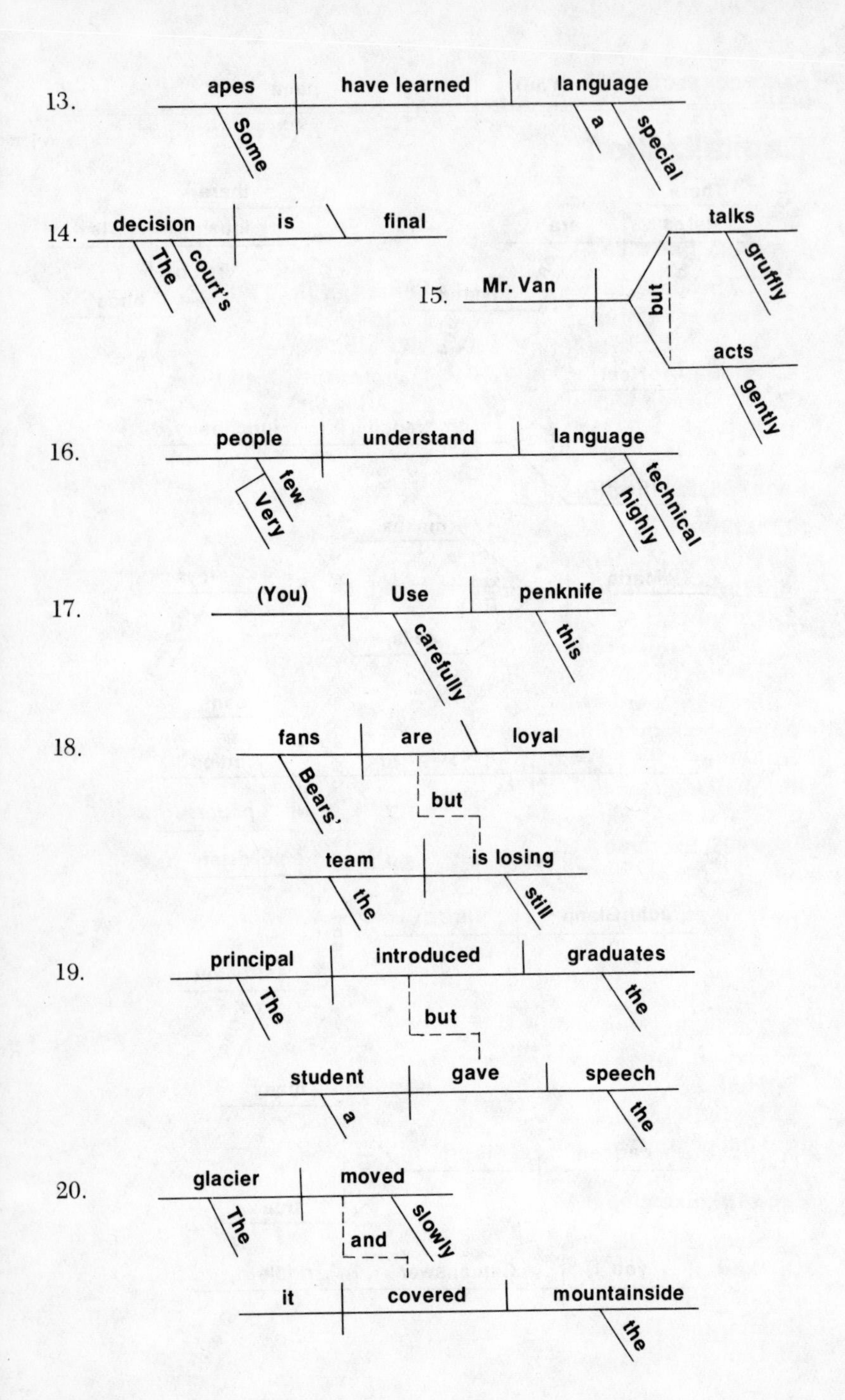
13.
apes
have learned
language
Some
a
special
14.
decision
is
final
The
court's
15.
Mr. Van
talks
gruffly
but
acts
gently
16.
people
understand
language
few
Very
technical
highly
17.
(You)
Use
penknife
carefully
this
18.
fans
are
loyal
Bears'
but
team
is losing
the
still
19.
principal
introduced
graduates
The
the
but
student
gave
speech
a
the
20.
glacier
moved
The
slowly
and
it
covered
mountainside
the

Capitalization

Page 408, Exercise A

1. I, Theodore Taylor
2. Spencer A. Marks
3. Thomas Edison
4. Nadine
5. Dr. George Washington Carver
6. Laura Ingalls Wilder
7. I, Kenny, Maria
8. Mr., Mrs. Torres
9. I, Professor Eileen Black
10. Dr. Adams

Page 408, Exercise B

1. William Brant, Red Jacket, Moses Cleaveland
2. I, Mr. Quinlan's
3. President Lincoln, Harriet Beecher Stowe
4. Dennis, Mr. Cage
5. Althea's, Mrs. Hartley
6. Cassius Clay, Muhammed Ali
7. Dr. Rosenberg, Italy
8. Senator Edward Kennedy
9. Lottie, I, Ms. Franklin's
10. Marian Anderson

Page 405, Exercise A

1. Easter
2. Long Island, New Jersey, World Trade Center
3. Amazon River, Brazil, Argentina
4. Dean's Dairy Bar
5. West, Arizona
6. Lazy K Ranch
7. Hawaii, King Kamehameha
8. Highway
9. Irwin Hospital, East
10. Gulf of Mexico

Page 410, Exercise B

1. South, Florida
2. West
3. Grand Tetons
4. Houston, Tuesday
5. Denver, Colorado

6. Golden Gate Bridge, San Francisco
7. Christmas, Colorado
8. Thanksgiving, Plimoth Plantation
9. Cathedral Square, Kremlin, Moscow
10. Puerto Rico, Thursday, July

Page 411, Exercise A

1. a Dutch windmill
2. African art
3. German potato salad
4. the Cub Scouts
5. Polish sausage
6. a Methodist minister
7. Chinese food
8. the Campfire Girls
9. Bell Telephone Company
10. the Arab oil fields

Page 411, Exercise B

1. Our school has language classes in French, Italian, and Spanish.
2. The Olmecs were an ancient Indian tribe in Mexico.
3. Gabriel joined the United States Marine Corps.
4. Were those tourists speaking Japanese?
5. Many people in India practice Hinduism.
6. Dolores's mother is a systems analyst for the Digital Equipment Company.
7. The Elmwood Photography Club meets every Monday in the Carnegie Library.
8. Roberto is active in the Peoria Chamber of Commerce.
9. The museum exhibits include an Egyptian mummy and several Roman statues.
10. The Irish writer Jonathan Swift wrote a great English novel about a man named Gulliver.

Page 413, Exercise A

1. The third Sunday in June is Father's Day.
2. Is cotton still an important crop in the South?
3. Listen, my children, and you shall hear
   Of the midnight ride of Paul Revere,
   On the eighteenth of April, in seventy-five;
   Hardly a man is now alive
   Who remembers that famous day and year.
4. Last year we had a dry summer and a rainy fall.
5. Do you like Italian food? We can have pizza at Tina's Restaurant.
6. There is a program on television tonight about Japan.
7. Dr. Frances Gilbert teaches English at Carroll University.
8. On Tuesday I will celebrate my birthday.
9. This month has five Saturdays.
10. Have you seen any movies by Woody Allen?

Page 413, Exercise B

1. The orchestra will play two works by Wolfgang Amadeus Mozart.
2. Mom is going to Dearborn, Michigan, on Friday.
3. On Wednesday I'll be late for dinner. The Girl Scouts are having a meeting at four o'clock.
4. What is the Spanish word for *hello*?
5. Our new address is 141 Miller Avenue.
6. We celebrate Flag Day on June 14.
7. Are you visiting Montreal, in Quebec? There, many Canadians speak French.
8. Yesterday Rabbi Silver spoke at the synagogue in Newton.
9. The setting of the book is Boston, Massachusetts.
10. The Rhinoceros
    The Rhino is a homely beast,
    For human eyes he's not a feast,
    But you and I will never know
    Why Nature chose to make him so,
    Farewell, farewell, you old rhinoceros,
    I'll stare at something less prepoceros.

Page 415, Exercise A

1. "Try these crutches," the doctor said.
2. She asked, "Is a violin a fiddle?"
3. "The pineapple is delicious," Stu said.
4. He asked, "Is Gordon a nurse?"
5. "Where is my mistake?" Amy asked.
6. The fortune teller said, "Pick a card."
7. Ms. Berg asked, "Where is your homework?"
8. Rona commented, "You're a good basketball player."
9. "The park is closed," the guard told us.
10. "Where is a salesperson?" the customer asked.

Page 415, Exercise B

1. Indians of the Northeast
    I. Groups
        A. Lake Indians
        B. Woodland Indians
    II. Important foods
        A. Lake Indians
            1. Wild rice
            2. Fish
        B. Woodland Indians
            1. Corn
            2. Deer and other game

2. Dear Kathleen,

Thank you for showing me the sights of Washington, D.C., last week. Nothing here in Chicago seems as exciting as the White House, the Capitol, or the Smithsonian Institution.

In one of my classes, I showed my photos of George Washington's home. We talked about the design of Mount Vernon and why it was built on the Potomac River. My teacher, Ms. Reynolds, asked about the small buildings surrounding the mainhouse. For once, I felt like an expert.

I hope that next July you will come to visit me. I'll make sure that you have a good time here in the Midwest.

Very truly yours,

Alison

Page 417, Exercise A

1. "Making Friends and Keeping Them"
2. *Teen*
3. "The Ransom of Red Chief"
4. *Star Trek*
5. "The Underwater World"
6. *Los Angeles Times*
7. "Dust of Snow"
8. "On Broadway"
9. "The Incredible Hulk"
10. *All Creatures Great and Small*

Page 417, Exercise B

1. "Battlestar Galactica"
2. *The Pigman*
3. *Superman*
4. "The Spirit of Democracy"
5. *Miami Herald*
6. "The Bat"
7. "To Build a Fire"
8. "Born Free"
9. *Time*
10. "What Do Your Dreams Mean?"

Page 418, Review

1. When is Barry Manilow's next concert?
2. Immediately, Judge Chase addressed the jury.
3. Jack's birthday is during the summer, but mine is November 8.
4. This Tuesday will be Groundhog Day.
5. Last winter Chicago, Illinois, had record snowfalls.
6. People attend bullfights in Madrid, Spain.
7. The two largest states are Texas and Alaska.
8. We met Mayor Minsky at City Hall.

9. Thornton Junior High is on Ridge Avenue.
10. The Snake River runs through a deep gorge.
11. Glacier National Park and Yellowstone National Park are in the West.
12. We traveled north to the Grand Canyon.
13. The Japanese welcomed Ambassador Graf.
14. The Catholic priest recited the prayer in Latin.
15. Did you play in the Lakeville Little League?
16. Ralston-Purina Company makes different animal foods.
17. "Here is the Royal Gorge Bridge," the guide said.
18. Bill asked, "Have you ever had a Greek salad?"
19. I read both *The Outsiders* and *That Was Then, This Is Now.*
20. "The Swan" is a poem by W. R. Rodgers.

HANDBOOK SECTION 17

Punctuation

Page 422, Exercise A

1. 4 ft. 10 in.
2. Washington, D.C.
3. 1 c. sugar
4. Bedford Ave.
5. Aug. 30
6. Butterford Chocolate Co., Inc.
7. Dr. H. M. Ritchie
8. Los Angeles, CA 90053
9. First five presidents
    1. George Washington
    2. John Adams
    3. Thomas Jefferson
    4. James Madison
    5. James Monroe
10. Super-8 movie-making
    I. Major equipment needed
        A. Camera
            1. For silent movies
            2. For sound movies
        B. Projector
    II. Other materials needed
        A. Film
        B. Splicer

Page 423, Exercise B

1. E.S.T.
2. N.Y., NY (or N.Y.)
3. Rev. J. Marsh
4. 4 gal.
5. Mt. Snow
6. Raleigh, N.C. (or NC)
7. Dec. 9
8. Benander Game Co.
9. 10 sq. ft.
10. Durapools, Inc.

Page 423, Exercise C

Answers will vary.

Page 424, Exercise A

1. Mr. and Mrs. Gregory go to Miami every winter.
2. Ouch! This pan is hot!
3. Dr. Evans will be in his office until 4:30.
4. What circus did P.T. Barnum manage?
5. Ms. Carol F. Kiley will speak at the N.H.S. graduation.
6. My new address is 600 W. 24 St.
7. Don't touch that broken glass!
8. We stopped at an L.C. Carran gas station.
9. How many Coke bottles are you returning?
10. Help! The gearshift is stuck in reverse!

Page 425, Exercise B

1. Terrific! We got the last four tickets.
2. How much does that album cost?
3. W.E.B. DuBois was a writer and a professor of sociology.
4. Jump out of the way of that car!
5. Mail the letter to Miss Deborah K. Sobol.
6. Is Dr. Howard your dentist?
7. The poet Hilda Dolittle signed her poems H.D.
8. Oh, no! You didn't forget the picnic lunch, did you?
9. Did Vanessa try out for the team last night?
10. We met Dr. Rusnak at her cousin's home.

Page 426, Exercise A

1. Yes, we went to the zoo last summer.
2. You can take a bus to the zoo, but we drove there.
3. We took our lunches, and we spent the whole day.
4. We saw a hippopotamus, a gorilla, and an anteater.
5. Since the zoo was built, two buildings have been added.
6. After the seals performed, they were fed by their trainer.
7. There were monkeys of every size, color, and shape.
8. Two monkeys started a fight, and another watched.
9. We took pictures, had a boat ride, and saw a movie.

10. The movie was good, but it wasn't as much fun as the animals at the zoo.

Page 427, Exercise B

1. No, it's not raining.
2. Karen aimed, fired, and just missed the bull's eye.
3. Motels are all right, but I like campgrounds better.
4. Robert and Anna weeded the garden, and Doug and Nancy repaired the fence.
5. Although it was raining, we still went swimming.
6. Denmark, Norway, and Sweden are called Scandinavian countries.
7. Will you drive us, or should we take the bus?
8. The spaghetti, tomato sauce, and spices are in that cupboard.
9. Because Joe was sick, he missed the test.
10. My sisters' names are Linda, Donna, and Jean.

Page 428, Exercise A

1. Last summer we went to Phoenix, Arizona.
2. Friday, May 5, was our opening night.
3. We all met the new principal, Mrs. Gomez.
4. At Kitty Hawk, North Carolina, the Wright brothers successfully flew three gliders.
5. Dad, this is Al Cresco, a friend of mine.
6. It was hot in Corpus Christi, Texas.
7. Hold the line, Gerry, and I'll ask her.
8. On Saturday, January 25, the excavation was begun.
9. Joey and Sandra, lunch is ready.
10. The famous comedian, Charlie Chaplin, accepted the award.

Page 428, Exercise B

1. Rhonda, were you born in September, 1968?
2. Albany, New York, is on the Hudson River.
3. Mary Shelley's famous novel, *Frankenstein,* was published in 1818.
4. Mr. Gray, let's have the exhibit on Friday, February 19.
5. The candidate, Ms. Wingreen, made a speech.
6. On October 4, 1957, the Soviet Union launched the first satellite.
7. You know, Adele, I'll be away tomorrow.
8. In Duluth, Minnesota, there is a statue of Jay Cooke, the financier.
9. No, Mrs. Lucas, I have never lived in Dayton, Ohio.
10. On October 7, 1943, my father was born.

Page 429, Exercise C

Sentences will vary.

Page 431, Exercise A

1. Benjamin said, "I'd like to visit Boston some day."
2. "This cake is delicious," said my father.
3. When Sheila typed, the table shook.
4. "It seems to me," Carol said, "that this puzzle is missing some pieces."
5. In the story, books were forbidden.
6. After we ate, the neighbors came to visit.
7. "Who," the caterpillar asked Alice in Wonderland, "are you?"
8. According to the paper, cups of coffee will cost a dollar each.
9. In the garden, flowers were blooming from May through September.
10. "Come here, Midnight," Ned called.

Page 432, Exercise B

1. While Vickie painted, Eric sanded the table.
2. "Tomorrow's weather," the forecaster said, "will be sunny and warm."
3. For dinner Tony had spaghetti, a salad, and dessert.
4. Ms. Miller announced, "The concert begins at seven o'clock."
5. "The radio is too loud," my mother complained.
6. When our team lost, the players felt depressed.
7. In the kitchen, chairs were rearranged.
8. Yvette asked, "What's on TV tonight?"
9. After Mr. Knowles left, his puppy whined.
10. "Three weeks ago today," Meg said, "I got my new bike."

Page 433, Exercise A

1. the girl's sweater
2. mechanics' tools
3. bird's nest
4. babies' toys
5. announcer's voice
6. goalies' saves
7. Chris's lunch
8. golfer's shots
9. children's games
10. family's vacation

Page 433, Exercise B

1. hunters'
2. Ms. Smith's
3. policemen's
4. women's
5. Louisa's
6. poets'
7. painter's
8. cats'
9. horse's
10. cyclist's
11. Dr. Bliss's
12. partner's

Page 434, Exercise A

1. I'm
2. aren't
3. it's
4. won't
5. hasn't
6. I'll
7. she's
8. we'd
9. we'll
10. isn't
11. that's
12. hadn't

Page 435, Exercise B

1. It's your turn, Joy.
2. We're waiting for Amy.
3. Darren can't come out this afternoon.
4. I haven't delivered the paper yet.
5. Wanda and Mike said that they're coming tomorrow.
6. Who's going to the library soon?
7. I'm ready to go.
8. It's too bad your dog hurt its leg.
9. What's your name?
10. I wish I'd been there.

Page 436, Exercise A

1. forty-five minutes
2. the fifty-ninth correction (or correction)
3. the Twenty-Second Amendment
4. thirty-four years
5. eighty-one trailers
6. seventy-nine years ago
7. ninety-three skateboards
8. twenty-nine cents
9. the sixty-fourth experiment (or experiment) (or experiment)
10. forty clarinets (or clarinets)

Page 436, Exercise B

1. the eighty-fifth problem
2. the forty-eighth state
3. the seventy-first variation (or variation) (or variation)
4. the twenty-two classrooms
5. ninety-seven cups
6. the fifty-fourth contestant (or contestant)
7. seventy-nine students
8. the thirty-sixth card
9. your ninety-third birthday
10. the twenty-ninth story

Page 438, Exercise A

1. "Drop anchor," bellowed the captain.
2. "Don't forget your key, Jeff," said Nina.
3. The cashier asked, "Will there be anything else?"
4. "Call me when you finish," said Ms. Walters.
5. Kevin replied, "I am finished now."

6. "My parents have already said I can't go," Pablo complained.
7. "Do you really believe in ESP?" asked Tammy.
8. Did Lillian say, "I'll be at the pool soon"?
9. Ron asked, "Where are you going?"
10. "Two eggs, with bacon!" shouted the waitress.

Page 438, Exercise B

1. "What was that noise?" asked my sister.
2. "Last call for dinner!" announced the Amtrak waiter.
3. "How can you eat so much pie, Willie?" Anita inquired.
4. "Those ears of corn look too big for that basket," Mr. Valdez remarked.
5. "What a tackle!" shouted David.
6. Mary said, "The roof is leaking."
7. "Who's there?" called Michelle.
8. Kathy's mother said, "I will help you."
9. "Watch the derrick!" Manny cried.
10. "Heavens to Betsy!" exclaimed Mrs. Mulligan.

Page 439, Exercise A

1. "Are you ready?" said Bryan. "I'll time you."
2. "The crawl kick isn't hard," Judy assured us. "Just keep your knees straight as you swim."
3. "Take the game home," Sally said generously. "You can keep it."
4. "How much does this spray cost?" Bonita inquired. "Is it guaranteed to repel mosquitoes?"
5. "What would you do," Mr. Rocher asked, "if the rope broke?"
6. "Before you leave," said Ms. Schafer, "I want you to finish this assignment."
7. "Where did you go?" Juanita asked. "I couldn't find you."
8. "Look at my watch!" exclaimed Sam. "It doesn't even have water in it."
9. "You can pat Prince," said Louise. "He won't bite."
10. "The other way," Hector insisted, "is much shorter."

Page 440, Exercise B

1. "Be careful!" shouted John. "The canoe will hit bottom."
2. "Ask Mrs. Mitchell," suggested Maureen. "Maybe we can broadcast the announcement."
3. "No," answered Seth, "my jacket is blue."
4. "If you need more spigots," said the farmer, "they're in this sap bucket."
5. "Fortunately," piped up Andrea, "I've got fifty cents."
6. "Turn the box over," my brother suggested. "Maybe the price is on the back."

7. "Saturday," Dora said, "I'll come about 8:30."
8. "I'm getting cold," shivered Robin. "Let's go in."
9. "The most interesting castles," Beth said, "were in Europe."
10. "Don't worry," said my mother. "It will wash out."

Page 441, Exercise

Fay and Alan looked at the lists of ice cream flavors at Swenson's Dairy.

"Have you made up your mind yet?" Fay asked.

"Yes," Alan said, "I'm getting strawberry."

"You always get strawberry," Fay said. "Why don't you ever try something new? I'm trying to decide between chocolate fudge and cherry ripple."

"That's why I always get strawberry," Alan said. "It's so much faster."

Page 442, Exercise A

1. *Close Encounters of the Third Kind*
2. *The Ark*
3. *Boston Globe*
4. "Child on Top of a Greenhouse"
5. "Football's Superstars"
6. *Field and Stream*
7. "M*A*S*H"
8. "The Age of the Glaciers"
9. "You Light Up My Life"
10. "The Tiger's Heart"

Page 442, Exercise B

1. *How the West Was Won*
2. "The Outcasts of Poker Flat"
3. *Call It Courage*
4. "The Diet That's Right for You"
5. "I'm Nobody! Who Are You?"
6. "The Undersea World of Jacques Cousteau"
7. *National Geographic*
8. *St. Louis Post-Dispatch*
9. "Ease On Down"
10. "Modern Art"

Page 443, Review

1. We will attend S.E. Grover High School.
2. Have you seen Dr. J.L. Pollock?
3. Meet me at school at 9 A.M.

4. Will you read my poem, Mr. Krause?
5. Wow! That's terrific!
6. Melinda said, "I rode on the trail near the lake."
7. Yes, I'd like to go to Disney World, Vicky.
8. Angie likes Andy Gibb, and she has many posters of him.
9. Dan Pierce, the manager, flew to Miami, Florida.
10. The treaty was signed on December 10, 1898.
11. My two brothers' bikes are identical.
12. Tina's excuse is better than yours, isn't it?
13. California hasn't had rain in months.
14. The women's club held its weekly meeting.
15. Who's pitching for the Cardinals today?
16. Carl said, "I'll run for office."
17. The man shouted, "Get out!"
18. Did she say, "No one cares"?
19. "Behind the painting," Dad said, "is our wall safe."
20. Gail said that she liked the poem "The Harbor."

HANDBOOK SECTION 18

Spelling

Page 447, Exercise

1. famous, lonely
2. having, argument
3. hoping
4. useful, changing
5. statement, moving
6. blaming
7. arrangement, ninety
8. blazing, severely
9. daring, exciting
10. writing, achievement

Page 448, Exercise

1. employer
2. enjoyable
3. marriage
4. played
5. carrying
6. sneakiest
7. destroyer
8. sixtieth
9. saying
10. replies
11. hurried
12. holiness
13. easily
14. readiness
15. boyish

Page 448, Exercise

1. immobile
2. leanness
3. misinformed
4. awfully, uneasy
5. illegal
6. carefully, misspell

7. illegible
8. Ideally, disobey
9. disapproves, stubbornness
10. really, irresponsible

Page 449, Exercise

1. received
2. exceed
3. precedes
4. believed
5. brief
6. yielded, fierce
7. proceeded
8. ceiling
9. succeed, believe
10. chief, seized

Page 450, Exercise

1. leaped
2. fatter
3. beating
4. cooler
5. chopper
6. hemmed
7. screaming
8. flapped
9. hotter
10. hugging
11. hearing
12. tripped
13. swimmer
14. leaping
15. peeked

Page 454, Exercise A

1. their
2. led
3. Whose
4. all ready
5. knew
6. lose
7. its
8. right
9. accept
10. quiet
11. Capitol
12. no
13. your
14. whether
15. piece

Page 455, Exercise B

1. write
2. loose
3. principal
4. plain
5. they're
6. lead
7. know
8. hear
9. you're
10. too
11. who's
12. new
13. capital
14. it's
15. except

Page 456, Review

1. hopeful
2. cities
3. carried, groceries
4. really, unsteady
5. meanness, surprising
6. succeed
7. ceiling
8. usually retrieves
9. spotted, misspelled
10. unnecessary
11. except
12. all ready
13. hear
14. new
15. led
16. loose
17. plain
18. write
19. their
20. you're